TEXAS LITERATURE: A CASE STUDY

With an Introduction
by Dagoberto Gilb

BEDFORD / ST. MARTIN'S   Boston ◆ New York

For Bedford/St. Martin's

Executive Developmental Editor: Ellen Thibault
Developmental Editor: Stephanie Naudin
Editor: Christina Gerogiannis
Production Editor: Kerri A. Cardone
Production Supervisor: Jennifer Peterson
Marketing Manager: Adrienne Petsick
Editorial Assistant: Sophia Snyder
Copyeditor: Mary Sanger
Project Management: Books By Design, Inc.
Text Design: Claire Seng-Niemoeller
Cover Design: Billy Boardman
Cover Art: *Texas State Fair Ferris Wheel, Dallas, Texas, USA* © Walter Bibikow/JAI/Corbis.
Composition: Books By Design, Inc.
Printing and Binding: Haddon Craftsmen, Inc., an RR Donnelley & Sons Company

President: Joan E. Feinberg
Editorial Director: Denise B. Wydra
Director of Marketing: Karen R. Soeltz
Director of Editing, Design, and Production: Marcia Cohen
Assistant Director of Editing, Design, and Production: Elise S. Kaiser
Managing Editor: Elizabeth M. Schaaf

Library of Congress Control Number: 2009920434

For information, write: Bedford/St. Martin's, 75 Arlington Street, Boston, MA 02116 (617-399-4000)

ISBN-10: 0-312-57604-8
ISBN-13: 978-0-312-57604-2

Acknowledgments

Gloria Anzaldúa. "To live in the Borderlands means you" and "The Homeland, Aztlán: El otro México" from *Borderlands/LaFrontera: The New Mestiza*. Copyright © 1987, 1999, 2007 by Gloria Anzaldúa. Reprinted by permission of Aunt Lute Books.

Rick Bass. "The Windy Day" from *The Lives of Rocks: Stories* by Rick Bass. Copyright © 2006 by Rick Bass. Reprinted by permission of Houghton Mifflin Harcourt Publishing Company. All rights reserved.

Contents

Illustrations

Introduction to This Collection

DAGOBERTO GILB

Dagoberto Gilb was born in Los Angeles and earned a BA and an MA from the University of California, Santa Barbara. When describing his background, Gilb told the *Los Angeles Times*, "My mother was Mexican, my father was of German descent. That's the future of this country. This kind of *mestizaje* is what we have, the culture we're creating." Gilb began working as a construction worker and journeyman carpenter after college and made a living for himself and his family for sixteen years, during which he kept a journal of his experiences and began publishing short fiction. Of how he found writing, Gilb said in an interview for identitytheory.com, "I saw it as an adventure. Writing was a physical adventure that I went through and recorded in a fictional way."

The Magic of Blood, a collection of Gilb's short stories, was first published in New Mexico in 1993. It won the 1994 PEN Hemingway Award, the

© Nancy Crampton. Used by permission.

I

Texas Institute of Letters Award for Fiction, and was a finalist for the PEN Faulkner Award. Other books by Gilb include *The Flowers, Gritos, Woodcuts of Women,* and *The Last Known Residence of Mickey Acuña.* He is the editor of *Hecho en Tejas: An Anthology of Texas Mexican Literature,* which is considered a major contribution to Texas literature. He has been translated and anthologized widely, and he has won various awards for his writing. He currently teaches in the Master of Fine Arts Creative Writing Program at Texas State University and lives in Austin, Texas.

¡Que Viva Texas!

Before it became the feed for many American stereotypes—and archetypes—that we who live here have to defend and deflect, what is now Texas was a territory where many now virtually unknown indigenous tribes wandered to and from its coasts and along its rivers and arroyos. Those native people enslaved the Spaniard Alvar Núñez Cabeza de Vaca, an officer on the shipwrecked Narváez voyage who'd been stranded on a journey of exploration and conquest and found himself on the coast of what is now Galveston Island. His *Relación,* or "Account," of those years is the first textually recorded tall tale that is set in Texas. Many explorers crossed from the south what we call the Rio Grande, and this land remained New Spain until the birth of the country of Mexico, making it the northern province of Coahuila y Tejas. Then a new force of people came from the west, and from places like Kentucky and Tennessee and Arkansas, linking it to the southern United States. In 1836, these latest inhabitants declared independence, and so it became the Republic of Texas, the nation of the lone star, for a decade. And so began, with those years, what is the glory and renown of its people and place: from the narratives of the Alamo, to the boom time in cattling and ranching and the lore of gunslinging outlaws and sheriffs; from oil wildcatters and rich tycoons, to the modern mediagenic stories of high-rolling business in Dallas and outer space mission control in Houston; to its famed and infamed politics on the Lyndon B. Johnson left and the George W. Bush right, the horror of the assassination of John F. Kennedy in between.

Literatures are often spoken of as encasing a country's cultural identity—think of French, German—or a continent's—African, Latin American. Is Irish literature British? Practically speaking it is, but to some it is no more so than Canadian would be. In the wide and large frame of American literature, publications from and set in the East Coast are tacitly accepted as national, while what lies beyond is called regional, as is the literature of the South, northern California, the Pacific Northwest, the Southwest, and so on, including Texas. Except *this* is Texas. If for no other reason than that it lasted ten years as a country all its own, "region" does not pertain to it. When J. Frank Dobie visited England, he went as a Texan. Larry McMurtry, who does not wear cowboy boots, might live in D.C., might write in Hollywood, but there's no doubt about his heritage. Where else could Molly

Ivins have gotten her loud humor? The border ballads chronicled by Américo Paredes could only be known alongside our long, legendary river.

Texas has always had these big stories, and the big voices to tell them, too. Several are included in this collection, names familiar across the country, like O. Henry, Barbara Jordan, Katherine Anne Porter, and Sandra Cisneros. But like much of the United States, Texas is changing its identity — again. If once upon a time it reflected the push away from a history south of the Rio Grande, the Mexican American community will soon represent 50 percent of the population here. Of all places, Texas has been the most ready for this, and of all places, it will become so uniquely. From its longtime adopted love of tacos, enchiladas, and open pit barbeque, to its adobe ranch-style architecture, to its love of color and light, Texas has long embraced its bicultural history. And so it will the new voices that will appear in the newest Texas, the ones who readers of this anthology will become.

Why is it that so many of our own go into a literature class with about as much enthusiasm as most do math or science? Why is it that so many think of those who love literature as being as socially dysfunctional as those who love physics or chemistry?

If I ask a young person to describe a poet or a writer, I commonly get a dreamy description of a very sophisticated man or woman, both with scarves twirled around their neck, keeping warm in a cold climate — probably standing in front of the Hudson or Charles River, or maybe at an Ivy campus, or even in Paris or London. And what do they write about? Stories that are intellectual adventures, written beside windows that have views from high above. If important, writers and poets, in other words, live elsewhere, away from the drawls and accents. They do not live here.

Have you ever noticed the joyful, exuberant passion that the Irish have for their literature? Doesn't every one of them know at least one poem by heart? Is it just some kind of native talent? No. It is because they know where they live and love where they live and have pride in who they are and what they do and how they survive. And so it is for us. What more forceful wind is there than the one that wants to blow down West Texas? What hotter sun than the one throbbing up over the Big Bend? What deeper blue than what carves out the Pecos River? What more powerful bright than a lightning storm in the Texas Hill Country? What the Irish understand is that by using their own words from their own land they embolden and nurture their soul. The soul? That oblong whatever-it-is that seems to usually inhabit an area in our body somewhere below our head and above our groin, though sometimes nearer the stomach, or liver, and so on. But your soul does its best artwork when the feet are touching home — when it and you are barefooted, mud squishing between the toes. That's when you're in Mercedes and looking up and seeing that it is *that* sky where the poem has been lurking, or when you're in Lubbock and hearing that wild cousin and knowing that *that* voice is telling the best story. It is when you are *here*, and *here* is Texas.

¡Que viva Texas! Onward and *adelante*!

—D. G.

Texas: A General Introduction

DON GRAHAM

Don Graham (b. 1940) is the author of several books about Texas and Texan literature, including *Kings of Texas: The 150-Year Saga of an American Ranching Empire, Giant Country: Essays on Texas, No Name on the Bullet: A Biography of Audie Murphy*, and *Cowboys and Cadillacs: How Hollywood Looks at Texas*. He graduated from North Texas State University in 1962 and earned his PhD in 1971 from the University of Texas, where he holds the position of J. Frank Dobie Regents Professor. In his book *Giant Country: Essays on Texas*, Graham speaks about what it is that any regional writer, in particular a Texan writer, seeks to achieve: "The task ... is to stop worrying about Texas as a provincial tag, a handicap, a brand. I'm interested in the gap between mythology and experience," he writes. "It's where I live, in Irony Gap." The following essay is the introduction to *Lone Star Literature: A Texas Anthology*, which he edited.

BEFORE YOU READ

In the following essay, Don Graham names a number of Texan writers who might surprise you. As you read, pay attention to how, according to Graham, Texas writing differs from the kind of writing produced in other states. Is there a particular style of writing unique to Texas?

Lone Star Literature: What Makes Texas Texas   *2003*

Stephen F. Austin, dreamer, impresario, father of Texas, and jailbird, made a most curious remark in a letter he wrote from his cell in Mexico City (February 6, 1835): "I hope that a dead calm will reign over Texas for many years to come — and that there will be no excitements whatever." His wish could hardly have been farther from the mark, for within a year Texas would be launched upon excitements enough to thrill the ages. In the space of a few months in the spring of 1836, Colonel William B. Travis, Davy Crockett, Jim Bowie, and a hundred and eighty or so other men died in defense of an old mission called the Alamo, in San Antonio; Colonel James W. Fannin's command was wiped out at Goliad; and Sam Houston's ragtag army vanquished Santa Anna at San Jacinto — all are the stuff of legend. The national press celebrated these events, and the mythmaking was off and running. It hasn't stopped since. Here is a brief list of what makes Texas *Texas*, besides the Alamo: (1) the Republic, (2) the Texas Rangers (the law enforcement agency, not the baseball team), (3) cattle drives, (4) King Ranch, (5) oil, (6) the Kennedy assassination, (7) LBJ, (8) movie/TV imagery, (9) George W. Bush.

The consequences for literature have been formidable mainly because both outsiders and sometimes Texans themselves often seem to expect if not prefer the stereotypes instead of the actual complexity and diversity of Texans. Most states aren't burdened by heavy accretions of myth. There is presumably no Iowa Mystique, for example. But all one has to do is say the word *Texas* and a host of clichés gallop into view: cowboys, vast plains, cattle, six-shooters, oil wells, big hair, etc. It is amazing how many people still derive their views of Texas from *Giant*, *The Last Picture Show*, and the TV show *Dallas*.

Although Texas is today largely an urban state with a population greater than that of Australia, many outsiders view it as a site of backwardness, yahoo manners, and a source of embarrassment. A commentary in the British magazine *The Economist* (April 4, 1998) is pretty typical of how Texas appears to visitors. A writer—probably British though no name was given—attended the Texas Book Festival, an annual event organized by Laura Bush when George W. was governor. The writer—let us call him/her "Anon"—had this to say about the reading habits of Texans: "Even educated Texans have often preferred insubstantial humour books and western pulp fiction to 'highfalutin' writing." Pass the grits, Ma. In point of fact, even the founding Texans were able to read and write. Astonishing but true. Sam Houston could recite yards of Alexander Pope's translation of *The Iliad*, and Mirabeau B. Lamar, second president of the Republic, wrote poetry. Not very good poetry, but verse nonetheless.

Not to pick too much on Anon, who is woefully uninformed, but less than a mile from the state capitol, where the festival was held, stands the Harry Ransom Humanities Research Center. It houses more British books and manuscripts by authors such as James Joyce, Virginia Woolf, and Samuel Beckett than Anon has doubtless ever seen or read.

Katherine Anne Porter, a Texas author not mentioned by Anon, illustrates a literary dimension of Texas that is sometimes overlooked. A writer of international renown, winner of the Pulitzer Prize and the National Book Award, and a native of Kyle, Texas, twenty miles south of Austin (her childhood home is now a national historical monument), Porter is not mentioned in Anon's learned account because (A) Anon is unaware of her Texas origins or (B) KAP does not fit the Texas stereotype, being a woman, not a cowgirl, and a Southern-oriented Texan, not a rancher's wife. To take her own interest in literature as one example of Texans' reading tastes, Porter, in 1915, in the sleepy little seacoast town of Corpus Christi, purchased a copy of *Tender Buttons*, Gertrude Stein's path-breaking volume of modernist prose. Books have a way of finding their audiences, even down in Texas.

Texas readers and writers have always read books from other cultures, other places. J. Frank Dobie, once the best known Texas writer, author of many of those books on topics that Anon would like to saddle all Texans as preoccupied with—longhorns, mustangs, rattlesnakes, vaqueros, etc.—read avidly, all his life. Among his constant favorites were the English Romantic poets and Victorian essayists. Larry McMurtry, the state's foremost author and intellectual, deals in fine books with a stock of 250,000 titles and has made his hometown of Archer City into a Texas version of Hay-on-Wye. McMurtry's home itself contains 21,000 volumes, and one room alone is filled with books about rivers. So not everybody in Texas is out in the barn yukking it up with crude humor books or dusty shoot-'em-ups. Not then, not now.

While the power of the mythology has been undoubtedly a problem for some Texas writers, causing them at times to write uncritically, to think in clichés and stereotypes, and to recycle local color for its own sake, a number of Texas writers have tapped into the stirring days of yesteryear to produce works of great quality. To name the most obvious, Larry McMurtry's *Lonesome Dove*, a glorious, gritty epic of the trail-drive era, stands first among Westerns and rivals classics such as *Moby Dick*. And of the hundreds of Alamo novels, Stephen Harrigan's *The Gates of the Alamo* goes a long way toward redeeming the obsession of writers and historians with the story of the old mission where Texas was paradoxically born out of blood and defeat. There are other novelistic appropriations of Texas history worth naming: Edwin Shrake's down-and-dirty recreation of Dallas in November 1963, recorded unflinchingly in *Strange Peaches*; John Graves's much admired narrative of a canoe trip into time, history, and nature, in *Goodbye to a River*; Cormac McCarthy's Melvillian masterpiece of American madness on the frontier in *Blood Meridian, Or the Evening Redness in the West*; James Carlos Blake's ultraviolent novel, *In the Rogue Blood*, which restages the Mexican War of 1846–1848; and Américo Paredes's excavation of the often ignored border troubles of 1914–1915 along the Rio Grande in South Texas, in *George Washington Gómez*. Numerous other titles might be brought forward as instances of writers working with Texas history in a highly inventive literary manner. Texas is a big space and we all have our favorites. . . .

"So Big" Texas. Following is the original caption that appeared on the back of this circa 1937 postcard: "The State of Texas is not only the largest but the most colorful in the U.S. Bordering on Mexico there was constant strife between the two nations. The Cavalcade of Texas is picturesque and colorful. Their bloody wars with Indians and Mexicans mark some of the outstanding struggles for Independence and existence in America. To the Texas Rangers and hardy citizens of the state go the credit for what may be called a Nation within a Nation — THE TEXANS. It is a state quite capable of living upon its own resources."
© Lake County Museum/Corbis.

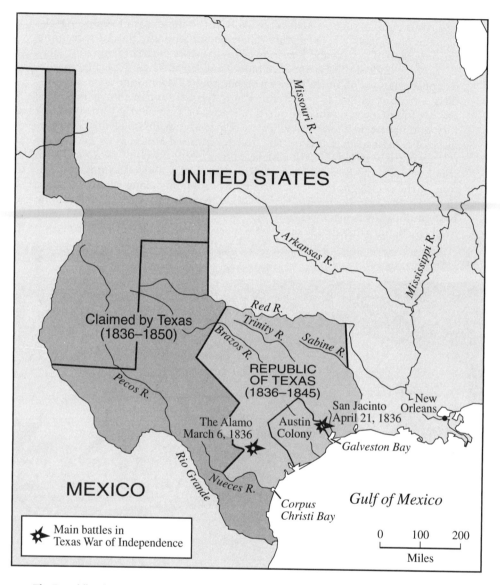

The Republic of Texas. Shown here are American settlements in Texas and landmark battles of the war of independence against Mexico.

Stephen F. Austin and Texas Colonists, 1823. Stephen F. Austin, the "Father of Texas," was the first American to colonize Spanish (and then Mexican) Texas. In this mural, he is pictured standing to the left of Baron de Bastrop (seated), the land commissioner of the Mexican government, as they discuss the partitioning of Texan land among the colonists.
© Bettmann/Corbis.

First Texas Oil Gusher, Spindletop Hill. An oil field in the southeast town of Beaumont sparked the beginning of the Texas oil industry and U.S. reliance on the state for a century's worth of energy to fuel planes, ships, and cars. Here residents gather at the site to witness the sideways gusher on January 10, 1901.
Getty Images.

JFK in Dallas Prior to Assassination (November 22, 1963). A few moments after this picture was taken, President John F. Kennedy was fatally shot by Lee Harvey Oswald. The president and First Lady Jacqueline Kennedy were in Dallas, Texas, as part of the 1964 reelection campaign.
© Corbis.

Lyndon B. Johnson in Johnson City (1908–1973). In 1960, Texas native Lyndon Baines Johnson (LBJ) was elected vice president of the United States as John F. Kennedy's running mate. After Kennedy's assassination, Johnson was sworn into office as president and served until 1969. This photo was taken on November 4, 1964, during a press barbecue on his Texas ranch.
© Bettmann/Corbis.

George W. Bush at the Alamo. This picture of Texas native George W. Bush was taken on August 1, 1998, when he was governor of the state. Two years later, he was elected president of the United States for two consecutive terms (2001–2009).
© Shepard Sherbell/Corbis.

[The dominant trend from 1860 to around the turn of the century] in American literature [was] Realism, an attempt to provide with photographic accuracy a true picture of modern life with its cities, railroads, and clash of titans, led by William Dean Howells. . . . Henry James, the recognized Master, published *The Ambassadors* [1903], another of his difficult novels about the clash between the Old World and the New, set in Paris.

The literature of Texas, however, was not yet ready to deal with the modern. The state was still close to the frontier. In [1900] warfare with the Plains Indians had been over for only twenty-six years, the cattle drives for eighteen years or so; the frontier was very much a part of the present, . . . down in Texas. And so the first literary efforts of the new century tended, not surprisingly, to sing of cowboys and cowboy songs, of the long trail, of the excitements and perils of outdoor life lived on the back of a fast horse, and of women, new brides of the new frontiers, their lives pitched like a tuning fork to the keenest of divergences and affinities between women and men living in a harsh and challenging land. Texas was hard on women and horses, so the saying went.

[Texas literature of] the early twentieth century [was preoccupied] with the frontier in works ranging from O. Henry, the first commercially successful Texas writer to find a national audience, through the obscure but quite astonishing memoirist Gertrude Beasley. But modern writers are drawn to the nineteenth-century frontier as well, and so the frontier motif flickers like a constant flame through the decades.

QUESTIONS FOR CRITICAL THINKING AND WRITING

1. According to "Anon," what makes up the bulk of Texas literature? How does Graham refute Anon's claim?

2. Graham describes the beginnings of literary Texas in the context of the rest of American literature at the turn of the century. While much of American literature dealt with Realism and clashes between "the Old World and the New," Graham argues that Texas was "not yet ready to deal with the modern." How does he support his argument? Is his argument valid? Why or why not?

3. Despite the tendency of people to think of Texas as clichéd and unvaried, Texas literature has a long, exciting history from which to draw characters and subject matter. Figures from Sam Houston to George W. Bush have had an effect on the country as a whole and certainly on the imagination of Texan writers. With Graham's essay in mind, write a brief essay on how you believe old and recent Texas history, and the myths surrounding it, might focus or shape the work of a Texas writer.

MOLLY IVINS

Molly Ivins (1944–2007) was a syndicated political columnist whose work appeared in more than 300 newspapers. She worked at the *Houston Chronicle* and the *Star Tribune* before becoming coeditor of the *Texas Observer* and later a columnist for the *Dallas Times Herald*. Ivins was an outspoken reporter known for her wit and biting sarcasm. She took particular delight in writing about politics and politicians, nicknaming George W. Bush, a fellow Texas native, "Shrub." Her writing philosophy is best summed up in the lines from her last column, published in 2007: "Raise hell. Think of something to make the ridiculous look ridiculous." She died of breast cancer.

BEFORE YOU READ

In this essay, Ivins examines the personalities of Texans with an eye toward Texas public figures. As you read, ask yourself how the particular and sometimes peculiar history of Texas comes across in the attitudes of the people who live there. How does Texas mythology influence a Texan's character?

Texas on Everything   *2003*

I've spent much of my life trying, unsuccessfully, to explode the myths about Texas. One attempts to explain — with all goodwill, historical evidence, nasty statistics, and just a bow of recognition to our racism — that Texas is not *The Alamo* starring John Wayne. We're not *Giant*, we ain't a John Ford Western. The first real Texan I ever saw on TV was Boomhauer, the guy who's always drinking beer and you can't understand a word he says, on *King of the Hill*.

So, how come trying to explode myths about Texas always winds up reinforcing them? After all these years, I do not think it is my fault — the fact is, it's a damned peculiar place. Given all the horseshit, there's bound to be a pony in here somewhere. Just by trying to be honest about it, one accidentally underlines its sheer strangeness.

Here's the deal on Texas. It's big. So big there's about five distinct and different places here, separated from one another geologically, topologically, botanically, ethnically, culturally, and climatically. Hence our boring habit of specifying east, west, and south Texas, plus the Panhandle and the Hill Country. East Texas is 50 percent black and more like the Old South than the Old South is anymore. West Texas is, more or less, like *Giant*, except, like everyplace else in the state, it has an incurable tendency toward the tacky, and all the cowboys are brown. South Texas is 80 percent Hispanic and a weird amalgam of cultures. You get names now like Shannon Rodriguez, Hannah Gonzalez, and Tiffany Ruiz. Even the Anglos speak English with a Spanish accent. The Panhandle, which sticks up to damn-near Kansas, is High Plains, like one of those square states, Nebraska or the Dakotas, except more brown folks. The Hill Country, smack dab in the middle, resembles nothing else in the state.

Molly Ivins in Austin. Following is the original caption that appeared with this photo in 1991: "Newspaper columnist Molly Ivins, known for her rapier wit, gleefully flexing a fencing sword in front of the TX State Capitol."
Time & Life Pictures/Getty Images.

Plus, plopped on top of all this, we have three huge cities, all among the ten largest in the country. Houston is Los Angeles with the climate of Calcutta, Dallas is Dutch (clean, orderly, and conformist), while San Antonio is Monterey North. Many years ago I wrote of this state: "The reason the sky is bigger here is because there aren't any trees. The reason folks here eat grits is because they ain't got no taste. Cowboys mostly stink and it's hot, oh God, is it hot. . . . Texas is a mosaic of cultures, which overlap in several parts of the state, with the darker layers on the bottom. The cultures are black, Chicano, Southern, freak, suburban, and shitkicker. (Shitkicker is dominant.) They are all rotten for women." All that's changed in thirty years is that suburban is now dominant, shitkicker isn't so ugly as it once was, and the freaks are now Goths or something. So it could be argued we're becoming more civilized.

In fact, it was always easy to argue that: Texas has symphony orchestras and great universities and perfect jewels of art museums (mostly in Fort Worth, of all places). It has lots of people who birdwatch, write Ph.D. theses on esoteric subjects, and speak French, for chrissake. But what still makes Texas Texas is that it's ignorant, cantankerous, and ridiculously friendly. Texas is still resistant to Howard Johnson's, interstate highways, and some forms of phoniness. It is the place least likely to become a replica of everyplace else. It's authentically awful, comic, and weirdly charming all at the same time.

Culturally, Texans rather resemble both Alaskans (hunt, fish, hate government) and Australians (drink beer, hate snobs). "They said it was Texas kulcher, but it was only railroad gin" goes an old song by Johnny Winter. The food is quite good—Mexican, barbecue, chili, shrimp, and chicken-fried steak, an acquired taste. The music is country, blues, folk, mariachi, rockabilly, and everything else you can think of. Mexican music—*norteno, ranchero*—is poised to "cross over," as black music did in the 1950s.

If you want to understand George W. Bush—unlike his daddy, an unfortunate example of a truly Texas-identified citizen—you have to stretch your imagination around a weird Texas amalgam: religion, anti-intellectualism, and machismo. All big, deep strains here, but still an odd combination. Then add that Bush is just another li'l upper-class white boy out trying to prove he's tough.

The politics are probably the weirdest thing about Texas. The state has gone from one-party Democrat to one-party Republican in thirty years. Lyndon said when he signed the Civil Rights Act in 1964 that it cost the Democrats the South for two generations. Right on both counts. We like to think we're "past race" in Texas, but of course east Texas remains an ugly, glaring exception. After James Byrd, Jr. was dragged to death near Jasper, only one white politician attended his funeral—U.S. Senator Kay Bailey Hutchison. Dubya, then governor, put the kibosh on the anti-hate crimes bill named in his memory. (The deal-breaker for Bush was including gays and lesbians. At a meeting last year of the Texas Civil Liberties Union board, vicious hate crimes against gays in both Dallas and Houston were discussed. I asked the board member from Midland if they'd been having any trouble with gay-bashing out there. "Hell, honey," she said, with that disastrous frankness one can grow so fond of, "there's not a gay in Midland would come out of the closet for fear people would think they're a Democrat.") Among the various strains of Texas right-wingism (it is factually incorrect to call it conservatism) is some leftover loony Bircherism, now morphed into militias, country-club economic conservatism à la George Bush *père*, and the usual batty antigovernment strain. Of course, Texas grew on the tender mercies of the federal government—rural electrification, dams, generations of master pork-barrel politicians and vast subsidies to the oil and gas industry. But that has never interfered with Texans' touching but entirely erroneous belief that this is the Frontier, and that in the Old West every man pulled his own weight and depended on no one else. The myth of rugged individualism continues to afflict a generation raised entirely in suburbs with names like the Flowering Forest Hills of Lubbock.

The Fall of the Alamo. During the Texas Revolution, William Travis and his army were ordered to protect the Alamo of San Antonio. Recruits and soldiers were scarce and the Texan soldiers were outnumbered approximately 200 to 2,000 against the Mexican army of General Antonio López de Santa Anna. On March 6, 1836, after weeks of fighting, the Mexicans rushed into the fortress and the Alamo fell.

© Bettmann/Corbis.

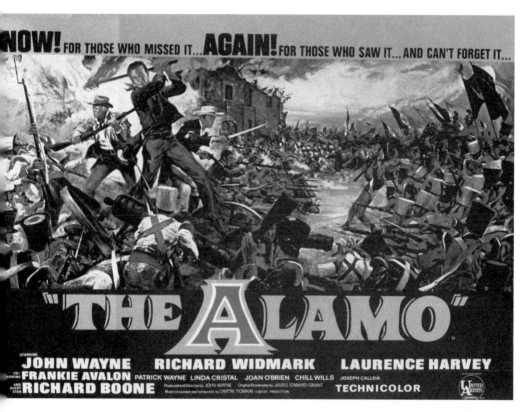

The Alamo. This 1960 film, John Wayne's directorial debut, dramatically recounts the happenings of the 1836 Battle of the Alamo.
United Artists/The Kobal Collection.

James Dean in *Giant* (1956). This Oscar-winning film was the last James Dean starred in. On September 30, 1955, the young actor died in a car crash while *Giant* was still in production. The movie, also starring Elizabeth Taylor, recounts the life of ranch owner Jordan "Bick" Benedict (Rock Hudson). When Bick's deceased sister leaves a piece of land to their arrogant neighbor, Jett Rink (James Dean), the cunning cowboy strikes oil and goes on to become one of the richest men in Texas.
© Bettmann/Corbis.

Boomhauer from *King of the Hill*. This nighttime cartoon comedy, which debuted on FOX in 1997, chronicles the life of Hank Hill, a Texan propane salesman. In the cartoon's regular opening scene, Bill ("Yep."), Hank ("Yep."), Dale ("Yep."), and Boomhauer ("Mmm-hmm.") discuss their personal problems and worldviews while drinking beer on the side of the road. Molly Ivins writes that Boomhauer (far right) was the "first real Texan" she ever saw on TV.
Fox Broadcasting/Photofest/© Fox Broadcasting.

South Texas. This photograph, taken in El Paso, Texas, illustrates the intermingling of the English and Spanish languages in southern Texas. As Molly Ivins writes in her essay, "South Texas is 80 percent Hispanic and a weird amalgam of cultures. . . . Even the Anglos speak English with a Spanish accent."

© Owen Franken/Corbis.

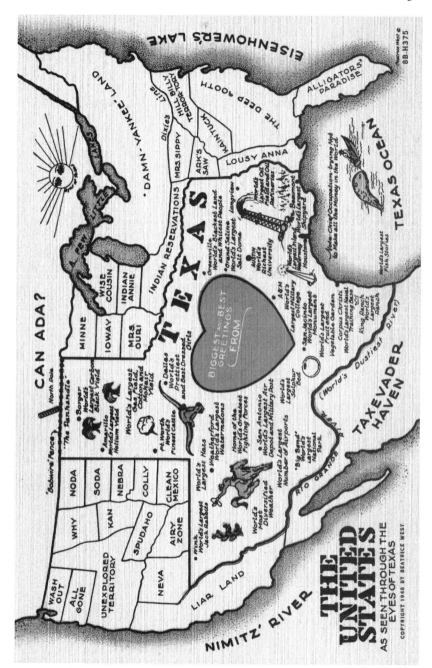

"The United States as Seen through the Eyes of Texas." This map, created in 1948 by Texan Beatrice West, is a satirical look at the country through the perspective of a Lone-Star-State native.
© Lake County Museum/Corbis.

The Populist movement was born in the Texas Hill Country, as genuinely democratic an uprising as this country has ever known. It produced legendary politicians for generations, including Ralph Yarborough, Sam Rayburn, Lyndon, and even into the nineties with Agriculture Commissioner Jim Hightower. I think it is not gone, but only sleeping.

Texans retain an exaggerated sense of state identification, routinely identifying themselves when abroad as Texans, rather than Americans or from the United States. That aggravated provincialism has three sources. First, the state is so big (though not as big as Alaska, as they are sure to remind us) that it can take a couple of days' hard travel just to get out of it. Second, we reinforce the sense of difference by requiring kids to study Texas history, including its ten years as an independent country. In state colleges, the course in Texas government is mandatory. Third, even national advertising campaigns pitch brands with a Texas accent here and certain products, like the pickup truck, are almost invariably sold with a Texas pitch. (Makes sense, with four times as many pickup drivers here as elsewhere.)

The founding myth is the Alamo. I was raised on the Revised Standard Version, which holds that while it was stupid of Travis and the gang to be there at all (Sam Houston told them to get the hell out), it was still an amazing last stand. Stephen Harrigan in *The Gates of the Alamo* is closer to reality, but even he admits in the end there was something romantic and even noble about the episode, rather like having served in the Abraham Lincoln Brigade during the Spanish Civil War.

According to the demographers at Texas A&M (itself a source of much Texas lore), Texas will become "majority minority" in 2008. Unfortunately, we won't see it in the voting patterns for at least a generation, and by then the Republicans will have the state so tied up by redistricting (currently the subject of a massive standoff in the legislature), it's unlikely to shift for another generation beyond that. The Christian Right is heavily dominant in the Texas Republican party. It was the genius of Karl Rove/George W. Bush to straddle the divide between the Christian Right and the country-club conservatives, which is actually a significant class split. The politics of resentment play a large role in the Christian Right: fundamentalists are perfectly aware that they are held in contempt by "the intellectuals." (In 1898 William Brann of Waco observed, "The trouble with our Texas Baptists is that we do not hold them under water long enough." He was shot to death by an irate Baptist.) In Texas, "intellectual" is often used as a synonym for "snob": George W. Bush perfectly exemplifies that attitude.

Here in the National Laboratory for Bad Government, we have an antiquated and regressive tax structure—high property, high sales, no income tax. We consistently rank near the bottom of every measure of social service, education, and quality of life (leading to one of our state mottoes, "Thank God for Mississippi"). Yet the state is incredibly rich in more than natural resources. The economy is now fully diversified, so plunges in the oil market can no longer throw the state into the bust cycle.

It is widely believed in Texas that the highest purpose of government is to create "a healthy bidness climate." The legislature is so dominated by special interests that the gallery where the lobbyists sit is called "the owners' box." The consequences of unregulated capitalism and of special interests being able to buy government through campaign contributions are more evident here because Texas is "first and worst" in this area. That Enron was a Texas company is no accident: Texas was also ground zero in the savings-and-loan scandal, is continually the site of major rip-offs by the insurance industry, and has a rich history of gigantic chicanery going way back. Leland Beatty calls Enron "Billie Sol Estes Goes to College." Economists call it "control fraud" when a corporation is rotten from the head down. I sometimes think Texas government is a case of control fraud too.

We are currently saddled with a right-wing-ideologue sugar daddy, James Leininger out of San Antonio, who gives immense campaign contributions and wants school vouchers, abstinence education, and the like in return. The result is a crew of breathtakingly right-wing legislators. This session, Representative Debbie Riddle of Houston said during a hearing, "Where did this idea come from that everybody deserves free education, free medical care, free whatever? It comes from Moscow, from Russia. It comes straight out of the pit of hell."

Texans for Lawsuit Reform, aka the bidness lobby, is a major player and has effectively eviscerated the judiciary with a two-pronged attack. While round after round of "tort reform" was shoved through the legislature, closing off access to the courts and protecting corporations from liability for their misdeeds, Karl Rove was busy electing all nine state supreme court justices. So even if you should somehow manage to get into court, you are faced with a bench noted for its canine fidelity to corporate special interests.

Here's how we make progress in Texas. Two summers ago, Governor Goodhair Perry (the man has a head of hair every Texan can be proud of, regardless of party) appointed an Enron executive to the Public Utilities Commission. The next day, Governor Goodhair got a $25,000 check from Ken Lay. Some thought there might be a connection. The guv was forced to hold a press conference at which he explained the whole thing was "totally coincidental." So that was a big relief. We don't have a sunshine law in Texas; it's more like a "partly cloudy law," but even here a major state appointee has to fill out a bunch of forms that are then public record. When the governor's office put out the forms on the Enron guy, members of the press, that alert guardian watchdog of democracy, noticed that number 17 looked funny. The governor's office had whited out the answers to question 17. A sophisticated cover-up.

Turns out 17 is the question about any unfortunate involvement with law enforcement. The alert guardian watchdogs were on the trail. We soon uncovered a couple of minor traffic violations and the following item. While out hunting a few years earlier, the Enron guy accidentally shot a whooping crane. Then he accidentally buried it, and as a result had to pay a $15,000 fine under what is known in Texas as the In Danger Species Act. We print this. A state full of sympathetic hunters reacted with, "Hell, anybody could accidentally shoot a whooper." But the press stayed on the story and was able to report the guy shot the whooper while on a goose hunt. Now the whooper is a large bird—runs up to five feet tall. The goose—short. Now we have a state full of hunters saying, "Hell, if this boy is too dumb to tell a whooper from a goose, maybe he shouldn't be regulatin' public utilities." He was forced to resign.

As Willie Nelson sings, if we couldn't laugh, we would all go insane. This is our redeeming social value and perhaps our one gift to progressives outside our borders. We do laugh. We have no choice. We have to have fun while trying to stave off the forces of darkness because we hardly ever win so it's the only fun we get to have. We find beer and imagination helpful. The Billion Bubba March, the Spam-O-Rama, the time we mooned the Klan, being embedded with the troops at the Holiday Inn in Ardmore, Oklahoma, singing "I Am Just an Asshole from El Paso" with Kinky Friedman and the Texas Jewboys, and "Up Against the Wall You Redneck Mother" with Ray Wylie Hubbard laughing at the loonies in the Lege—does it get better than this? The late Bill Kugle of Athens is buried in the Texas State Cemetery. On the front of his stone are listed his service in the Marines in World War II, his years in the legislature, other titles and honors. On the back of the stone is, "He never voted for a Republican and never had much to do with them either."

We have lost some great freedom fighters in Texas during the past year [2003]. Billie Carr, the great Houston political organizer (you'd've loved her: she got invited to the White House during the middle of the Monica mess, sashayed through the receiving line, looked Bill Clinton in the eye and said, "You dumb son of a bitch"), always said she wanted her funeral to be like her whole life in politics: it should start half an hour late, she wanted a balanced delegation of pallbearers—one black, one brown, two women—she wanted an open casket, and a name tag stuck over her left tit that said, "Hi there! My name is Billie Carr." We did it all for her.

At the funeral of Malcolm McGregor, the beloved legislator and bibliophile from El Paso, we heard "The Eyes of Texas" and the Aggie War Hymn played on the bagpipes. At the service for Maury Maverick, Jr., of San Antonio, at his request, J. Frank Dobie's poem "The Mustangs" was read by the poet Naomi Shihab Nye. The last stanza is:

So sometimes yet, in the realities of silence and solitude,
For a few people unhampered a while by things,
The mustangs walk out with dawn, stand high, then
Sweep away, wild with sheer life, and free, free, free—
Free of all confines of time and flesh.

QUESTIONS FOR CRITICAL THINKING AND WRITING

1. Ivins states that Texans are "ignorant, cantankerous, and ridiculously friendly." Which public figures mentioned in this essay reflect her view? How so?

2. Texas, according to Ivins, "is the place least likely to become a replica of everyplace else." What sorts of things homogenize the rest of the country, making it like "everyplace else"? Why, according to Ivins, is Texas resistant to homogenization?

3. Ivins ends her essay with a description of two public figures, Billie Carr and Malcolm McGregor. Why does she do this? How does her choice affect your reading?

4. **CONNECT TO ANOTHER READING.** Texas's history is, as Don Graham writes in "Lone Star Literature" (p. 7), "the stuff of legend." Both Ivins and Graham write of the myths and stereotypes surrounding Texas. In her essay, Ivins focuses on Texas personalities and insists, "We're not *Giant*, we ain't a John Ford Western." Consider one of the individuals described by Ivins. How are the myths and stereotypes of Texas reflected in his or her character? In a brief essay, examine this individual through the lens of the arguments made by Graham and Ivins.

WALTER PRESCOTT WEBB

Walter Prescott Webb was a writer and historian who focused on the American West. He was born in 1888 and grew up on a family farm in Panola County. Over the course of his lifetime, Webb presided as president of the Mississippi Valley Historical Association, the American Historical Association, and the Texas State Historical Association. While president of the Texas State Historical Association, he developed an idea that became, in 1952, the *Handbook of Texas*. A professor at the University of Texas, Webb wrote or edited more than twenty books, most of which are about the state's history, including *The Great Plains* (from which this essay comes), *The Texas Rangers*, *The Great Frontier*, and *An Honest Preface*. Webb died near Austin in 1963.

BEFORE YOU READ

In the following essay, Webb outlines the difficulties faced by early immigrants to Texas while explaining how the colony of Stephen Austin, known as the "Father of Texas," flourished in the state. Who were the people and what were the cultures that the early immigrants came into contact with? What challenges of geography did they face?

The Texans Touch the Plains   *1931*

The dividing line between the East and the West cuts the state of Texas into two almost equal parts. As Colonel Marcy* pointed out, the Cross Timbers roughly marked the dividing line, which in this time separated civilized man from the savage. Below the Cross Timbers† the line veers to the southeast, touching the coast near the old town of Indianola. This brings it about that the country around San Antonio and southward from there partakes of the nature of the Plains. San Antonio was the Plains outpost of Spanish occupation. The Plains Indians raided around San Antonio and on to the coast throughout the open country, or wherever they could ride on horseback. The Mexicans were even less successful than the Spaniards had been.

In 1821 Stephen F. Austin introduced into Texas (then a Mexican province) a colony of immigrants from the United States. He did not, however, attempt to make his settlement near the Plains portion of the state; he chose that portion of the state which is in its nature very similar to the more fertile regions of the Mississippi Valley. Like the people who two decades later went to Oregon, he sought the timbered and well-watered environment, along the Brazos and Colorado rivers, in which the settlers he expected to introduce would feel

*Colonel Randolph Barnes Marcy (1812–1867) served as inspector general of the U.S. Army from 1871 to 1881. In 1849, he founded the Marcy Trail, leading 500 Arkansans across Comanche territory from Fort Smith, Arkansas, to Sante Fe, New Mexico.

†*Cross Timbers:* A narrow strip of land that runs from southeast Kansas through central Oklahoma and into central Texas.

at home. Austin's biographer has thus described the land that the empresario chose:

> Austin's boundaries included the fairest part of the province then known — land of exhaustless fertility, abundantly watered and accessible to the sea, timber and prairie interspersed in convenient proportions. . . . All who visited Texas and returned to the United States advertised its superior natural advantages, and men who had themselves no intention of emigrating wrote to Austin for reliable information which they might detail to others.

The other American contractors who followed Austin to Texas established themselves as near his colony as circumstances would permit. Although the strength of Austin's colony had something to do with this decision, the nature of the land probably had as much or more. The Americans were appropriating to themselves the agricultural lands lying along the middle courses of the rivers. It is significant that not one of these settlements lay west of the ninety-eighth meridian, and more significant that those which lay north and west of Austin's colony were in continual apprehension of the Indians.

Austin's relations with the Comanches are worth noting here, not because they were important but because they were significant. In March, 1822, he found it necessary to go from San Antonio to Mexico City on business. Between San Antonio and Laredo he came into the barren country, which pushes eastward in this section. He described it as the "poorest I ever saw in my life, it is generally nothing but sand, entirely void of timber, covered with scrubby thorn bushes and prickly pear." He declared Laredo to be "as poor as sand banks, and drought, and indolence can make it." These statements show that the careful and conservative Austin, who became the father of Texas, would have been repelled immediately had he been confronted with the necessity of making a settlement in this, a pure Plains environment. He had no experience that fitted him to live without timber and water.

As Austin went south he found that "between San Antonio and Monterrey the Indians were a continual menace." He was in the southern range of the Apaches and Comanches, and near the Nueces River he and his single companion were surrounded and captured by fifty Comanches, who seized all their belongings. But when the Comanches found that their captives were Americans and not Mexicans, they gave them their freedom and restored all their property except a bridle, four blankets (note that what they kept pertained to horses), and a Spanish grammar! Knowing the Comanches to be horsemen, we can easily understand their keeping the bridle and blankets, but just what they wanted with the Spanish grammar remains a mystery.

In applying for a grant to settle his "Little Colony," on the east bank of the Colorado, north and west of the original settlement, Austin declared that the people of San Antonio requested him to settle there to protect travelers and check Comanche and Tahuacano raids on San Antonio.

That Austin understood the Indian situation in Texas and the difference between a Plains Indian and a timber Indian is perfectly clear from a reading of his biography and letters. In eastern Texas were the generally peaceful Cherokees, Choctaws, and Caddos; among the settlers were the weak Tonkawas, and below them on the coast the ferocious but numerically weak Karankawas. To the west were the Wacos and Tahuacanos, who might be termed a semi-Plains people: they dwelt in the Prairie Plains, and although they cultivated crops they also rode horses and hunted the buffalo. Beyond these were the never-to-be-misunderstood Comanches.

Austin, always keenly alive to the practical policy that he should follow purely in reference to his own colony, did not fail to make good use of the Comanche's partiality for Americans. In connection with this subject Barker says:

> The desperate situation can be inferred from the embarrassing proposal which Austin made to the political chief for avoiding Comanche hostility in 1825. Rumor reported these Indians to he raiding San Antonio and Goliad, robbing and killing, but the settlers still profited from their partiality to Americans and were not disturbed. Though it shamed him to the soul, Austin suggested that they take advantage of this circumstance until they were strong enough to carry on an effective campaign. . . . [He] counseled the selfish policy of *sauve qui peut* until the settlement was on its feet.

Further light is thrown on the Texas Indian question by two orders which Austin received from the superior military officer in Texas. The first, dated

QUANAH PARKER· CHIEF OF COMANCHE INDIANS AND SQUAW TO-NICY.

Chief Quanah Parker. Quanah Parker (1850–1911), shown here with one of his wives, was the last chief of the Comanche Indians. He led raids on frontier settlements from 1867 to 1875 when he and his tribe finally surrendered. Parker founded the Native American Church Movement, which relied immensely on the medicine of peyote. He was also believed to be, at one time, the wealthiest Indian in the United States.
© Corbis.

August 21, 1825, ordered him to march at once against the Wacos, Tahuacanos, and Tahuiases; the second, dated five days later, countermanded the order because the Comanches were reported to be at the Waco villages in force. Both orders were received the same day. Austin, foreseeing a repetition of the first order, adroitly began to maneuver the Indian situation into his own hands; that is, he took the initiative and distributed a questionnaire among his people to ascertain the consensus of opinion concerning the policy that should be pursued. Should they go to war with the western Indians and leave the colony open to the incursions of the coast treaties? Should they ask the Tonkawas and Lipans (the eastern remnant of the Apaches and undying enemies of the Comanches) to join them? Should they fight or should they make treaties? With unerring skill Austin inserted the suggestion that it would be better to delay. Revenge should wait on the proper time, and that time should be determined by cool judgment and not by passion. In the meantime the colony would grow strong, and, besides, the Leftwich colony was about to be settled between them and the troublesome Indians and would serve as a buffer. Like a skillful parliamentarian Austin kept peace when both his colonists and the Mexican government wanted war. When he wrote a friend that the government was displeased that he had not gone to war, the friend replied that it was better to be driven from the country by the government than by the Indians.

Austin did not hesitate, however, to take strong measures against the Indians. In the winter following the incidents just related his settlement was entered by Choctaws in search of Tonkawas and by Tahuacanos on a horse-stealing expedition. The thieving Indians were attacked, and a number were killed. Austin now made preparations for an Indian campaign in May of 1826, and did exactly what the Spaniards had done in the previous century: he formed an alliance with the Cherokees, Shawnees, and Delawares; but the alliance was vetoed by the Mexican officials, and the campaign was suspended.

In the summer Austin called together the representatives of the various militia districts to adopt a plan by which to guard against the incursions of the Indians. "The result of this conference was an arrangement to keep from twenty to thirty mounted rangers in service all the time."

We do not know whether these rangers were called into service; but it does not matter, for the provision for them is significant. Austin had not settled his colony on the Plains, but he was near enough to the Plains to feel the influence of the Plains Indians, who always came and went on horseback. It is to be noted that the most serious trouble came from the west, and that this trouble had brought into embryo the organization of the Texas Rangers, later to be perfected and developed into a mounted fighting organization whose reputation has spread over the English-speaking world and is intimately known by at least one Latin nation. Just as the explorers who set out from Missouri to cross the Plains had to leave their boats and take to wagons and horses, so the Texans found it necessary to mount their horses in order to meet the mounted Plains Indians. The Texans still had to learn much about horses and horseback fighting, but they had no choice in the matter, if they were to succeed in their contest with the Indians for possession of the Plains.

It is not the purpose here to follow in detail the spread of Austin's colony, the coming of other contractors and immigrants from the United States to Texas. As they came in they found it necessary to push north and west of the original settlements, debouching on the open Plains, where they came into contact and into conflict with the Plains Indians. At first they made no effort at permanent settlement in that direction, but clung almost instinctively to the woodland region. From 1821 to 1836 these venturesome Texans were the outriders of the American frontier. They had thrust a salient into the frontier of Mexico. They were still in a familiar physical environment, but they were so close to the borders of the new environment that its problems confronted them from the first. They could not go northwest, west, or southwest without coming into the range of the Comanches and other mounted Indians. They were also in contact with the Mexicans — not so much with the Mexican population as with the Mexican government, under which they had voluntarily placed themselves but with which they never found themselves in complete accord. Potentially, Texas was a center of three conflicting civilizations — that of the Mexicans, that of the Texans, and that of the Plains Indians. The potential conflict soon became a real one, eventuating in that tempestuous period beginning with the Texas revolution and ending with the Mexican War, between which events the Texans maintained an independent republic.

During the ten years of the republic Texas and the Texans had no peace. Mexico refused to recognize the independence of its lost province and maintained a constant threat of war which expressed itself in occasional partisan raids into Texas. San Antonio was twice captured by Mexican armies. The Texans also made two attacks against Mexico. In 1841 the Santa Fe expedition left Austin with the ostensible purpose of establishing the jurisdiction of Texas over Santa Fe and, if possible, of making good the claim of Texas to the upper Rio Grande valley. In 1842 a party of Texans set out to invade Mexico. Their disastrous venture is known as the Mier expedition, for the reason that when the Texans reached Mier they were captured by a Mexican army. Both the Santa Fe expedition and the Mier expedition ended in disaster, most of the participants being captured and some executed.

Out of their long experience with both Mexicans and Indians the Texans learned that they could never afford to surrender. The memory of what happened at the Alamo in 1836 affected the attitude of those who found themselves in conflict with the Mexicans. But the Mexicans were not the only foes who gave no quarter: the Plains Indians who dwelt in the West did not know the meaning of the word and were past masters in the art of human torture. Thus it came about that the Texans were confronted by two foes to neither of whom they could surrender: *they had to fight.*

It is a military axiom that an enemy imposes on his foe his own military methods, provided they be superior ones. The military methods of both the Plains Indians and the Mexicans had to do with horses. The Texas border war was not a warfare of pitched battles, but of great distances, sudden incursions, and rapid flight on horseback. The attackers always came on horseback, with an organization mobile and fleet and elusive. They had to be met and pursued on horseback with an organization equally mobile. Had Texas been populous and wealthy its task of defense would have been easy; but it had few men to enlist and nothing save land and paper money, equally worthless in Texas, to pay them with. Whatever fighting force Texas devised, therefore, must be small and economical as well as mobile and fleet. From these hard conditions was evolved the organization of the Texas Rangers. What these men had inherited and brought with them to the West was blended with what they acquired after their arrival into a type which was thus set forth by an understanding writer: "A Texas Ranger can ride like a Mexican, trail like an Indian, shoot like a Tennesseean, and fight like a very devil!"

QUESTIONS FOR CRITICAL THINKING AND WRITING

1. According to Webb, which of Stephen Austin's qualities made him a strong leader?

2. Webb writes of "two foes"—the Mexicans and the Indians—who confronted the Texans as they began to populate the state. Why did the immigrants think of Mexicans as their adversaries? The Indians?

3. During a time of struggle among the colonists, the Mexican government, and the Native Americans, a friend of Stephen Austin's is quoted as saying it would be "better to be driven from the country by government than by the Indians." Why did he say this?

4. **RESEARCH AND WRITE.** At one time, Native American tribes inhabited every region of what is now the American Southwest. Webb writes of the "Indian situation" in Texas and lists the many Indian peoples Austin's colony may have come into contact with. Research one of the Texas-based tribes mentioned in this essay that would have had contact with the early Texans. Write a brief summary of that people's worldview and their relationship with the Americans, the Mexicans, and other tribes who populated Texas.

A Collection
of Texas Literature

Gloria Anzaldúa

Gloria Anzaldúa (1942–2004) was born in the Rio Grande Valley of southern Texas. Anzaldúa, who described herself as "a Chicana *tejana* lesbian-feminist poet and fiction writer," graduated with a BA from Pan American University and an MA in comparative literature from the University of Texas at Austin. She moved to California in the 1970s to become a teacher and writer. She wrote and edited many books, including *This Bridge Called My Back: Writings by Radical Women of Color* (coedited with Cherríe Moraga); *Making*

Courtesy of Nettie Lee Benson Latin American Collection, University of Texas Libraries, The University of Texas at Austin.

Face, Making Soul/Haciendo Caras: Creative and Critical Perspectives by Feminists of Color; This Bridge We Call Home: Radical Visions for Transformation (with Analouise Keating); *Borderlands/La Frontera: The New Mestiza*; and various works of fiction, poetry, and children's literature. *Borderlands/La Frontera: The New Mestiza*, the book from which this poem comes, received recognition from *Utne Reader* and was named by *Hungry Mind Review* as one of 100 Best 20th-Century American Books of Fiction and Nonfiction. The term *new mestiza*, coined in the title, refers to Mexican Americans like Anzaldúa whose dual identities are in conflict yet who must blend with others to form a new, vital society.

Before You Read

In the following poem, Anzaldúa explores what it means to grow up in the borderlands of Texas. While you read, consider what effect living on the border between cultures and countries can have on the individual.

To live in the Borderlands means you   *1987*

>   are neither *hispana india negra española*
>   *ni gabacha,*° *eres mestiza, mulata,* half-breed
>   caught in the crossfire between camps
>   while carrying all five races on your back   5
>   not knowing which side to turn to, run from;
>
> To live in the Borderlands means knowing
>   that the *india* in you, betrayed for 500 years,
>   is no longer speaking to you,
>   that *mexicanas* call you *rajetas,*°   10
>   that denying the Anglo inside you
>   is as bad as having denied the Indian or Black;

2 *gabacha:* A Chicano term for a white woman.   10 *rajetas:* Literally, "split," that is, having betrayed your word.

Cuando vives en la frontera
    people walk through you, the wind steals your voice,
    you're a *burra,*° *buey,*° scapegoat,   15
    forerunner of a new race,
    half and half—both woman and man, neither—
    a new gender;

To live in the Borderlands means to
    put *chile* in the borscht,   20
    eat whole wheat *tortillas,*
    speak Tex-Mex with a Brooklyn accent;
    be stopped by *la migra* at the border checkpoints;

Living in the Borderlands means you fight hard to
    resist the gold elixer beckoning from the bottle,   25
    the pull of the gun barrel,
    the rope crushing the hollow of your throat;

In the Borderlands
    you are the battleground
    where enemies are kin to each other;   30
    you are at home, a stranger,
    the border disputes have been settled
    the volley of shots have shattered the truce
    you are wounded, lost in action
    dead, fighting back;   35

To live in the Borderlands means
    the mill with the razor white teeth wants to shred off
    your olive-red skin, crush out the kernel, your heart
    pound you pinch you roll you out
    smelling like white bread but dead;   40

To survive the Borderlands
    you must live *sin fronteras*°
    be a crossroads.

15 *burra, buey:* Donkey, oxen.   42 *sin fronteras:* Without borders.

QUESTIONS FOR CRITICAL THINKING AND WRITING

1. Why do you think Anzaldúa chooses to use two languages in this poem? What effect does the mix of English and Spanish have?

2. What do you think Anzaldúa is referring to when she says someone living in the borderlands is "caught in the crossfire between camps"?

3. In the second stanza, how many different races are identified as part of the borderlands? What point about race is Anzaldúa making in that stanza?

4. A crossroads is a place where roads intersect. Usually when people say they "come to a crossroads" in life, they are talking about a critical point at which a decision must be made. In a short essay, write about the image of the crossroads in Anzaldúa's poem. Is she speaking figuratively, literally, or both? In your reading of the poem, what do you think it means to *be* a crossroads?

GLORIA ANZALDÚA

For a biographical note on Gloria Anzaldúa, see page 37.

BEFORE YOU READ

In the following essay, Anzaldúa speaks of how the annexation of Texas and resulting border with Mexico shaped the lives of her family and other Mexican and indigenous people of the region. As you read, how do you understand the difficulties faced by those who live in, or who wish to return to, "the promised land" of Aztlán?

The Homeland, Aztlán: El otro México   *1987*

El otro México que acá hemos construido
el espacio es lo que ha sido
territorio nacional.
Esté el esfuerzo de todos nuestros hermanos
y latinoamericanos que han sabido
progressar.
        —*Los Tigres del Norte*[1]

"The *Aztecas del norte* . . . compose the largest single tribe or nation of Anishinabeg (Indians) found in the United States today. . . . Some call themselves Chicanos and see themselves as people whose true homeland is Aztlán [the U.S. Southwest]."[2]

Wind tugging at my sleeve
feet sinking into the sand
I stand at the edge where earth touches ocean
where the two overlap
a gentle coming together   5
at other times and places a violent clash.

  Across the border in Mexico
    stark silhouette of houses gutted by waves,
      cliffs crumbling into the sea,
        silver waves marbled with spume   10
          gashing a hole under the border fence.

        Miro el mar atacar
      la cerca en Border Field Park
     con sus buchones de agua,
an Easter Sunday resurrection   15
of the brown blood in my veins.

Oigo el llorido del mar, el respiro del aire,
  my heart surges to the beat of the sea.

In the gray haze of the sun
    the gulls' shrill cry of hunger,   20
        the tangy smell of the sea seeping into me.

        I walk   through the hole in the fence
            to the other side.
    Under my fingers I feel the gritty wire
        rusted by 139 years   25
            of the salty breath of the sea.

Beneath the iron sky
Mexican children kick their soccer ball across,
run after it, entering the U.S.

        I press my hand to the steel curtain —   30
    chainlink fence crowned with rolled barbed wire —
rippling from the sea where Tijuana touches San Diego
        unrolling over mountains
            and plains
                and deserts,   35
this "Tortilla Curtain" turning into *el río Grande*
    flowing down to the flatlands
        of the Magic Valley of South Texas
    its mouth emptying into the Gulf.

1,950 mile-long open wound   40
        dividing a *pueblo*, a culture,
        running down the length of my body,
            staking fence rods in my flesh,
        splits me   splits me
           me raja   *me raja*   45

        This is my home
        this thin edge of
        barbwire.

        But the skin of the earth is seamless.
        The sea cannot be fenced,   50
    el mar does not stop at borders.
To show the white man what she thought of his
               arrogance,
        Yemaya blew that wire fence down.

        This land was Mexican once,   55
            was Indian always
            and is.
        And   will be again.

Yo soy un puente tendido
    del mundo gabacho al del mojado,   60
lo pasado me estirá pa' 'trás
    y lo presente pa' 'delante.
Que la Virgen de Guadalupe me cuide
Ay ay ay, soy mexicana de este lado.

The U.S.-Mexico Border in El Paso, Texas.
© JP Laffont/Sygma/Corbis.

The U.S.-Mexican border *es una herida abierta* where the Third World grates against the first and bleeds. And before a scab forms it hemorrhages again, the lifeblood of two worlds merging to form a third country—a border culture. Borders are set up to define the places that are safe and unsafe, to distinguish *us* from *them*. A border is a dividing line, a narrow strip along a steep edge. A borderland is a vague and undetermined place created by the emotional residue of an unnatural boundary. It is in a constant state of transition. The prohibited and forbidden are its inhabitants. *Los atravesados* live here: the squint-eyed, the perverse, the queer, the troublesome, the mongrel, the mulato, the half-breed, the half dead; in short, those who cross over, pass over, or go through the confines of the "normal." Gringos in the U.S. Southwest consider the inhabitants of the borderlands transgressors, aliens—whether they possess documents or not, whether they're Chicanos, Indians or Blacks. Do not enter, trespassers will be raped, maimed, strangled, gassed, shot. The only "legitimate" inhabitants are those in power, the whites and those who align themselves with whites. Tension grips the inhabitants of the borderlands like a virus. Ambivalence and unrest reside there and death is no stranger.

> In the fields, *la migra*. My aunt saying, "*No corran*, don't run. They'll think you're *del otro lao*." In the confusion, Pedro ran, terrified of being caught. He couldn't speak English, couldn't tell them he was fifth generation American. *Sin papeles*—he did not carry his birth certificate to work in the fields. *La migra* took him away while we watched. *Se lo llevaron.* He tried to smile when he looked back at us, to raise his fist. But I saw the shame pushing his head down, I saw the terrible weight of shame hunch his shoulders. They deported him to Guadalajara by plane. The furthest he'd ever been to Mexico was Reynosa, a small border town opposite Hidalgo, Texas, not far from McAllen. Pedro walked all the way to the Valley. *Se lo llevaron sin un centavo al pobre. Se vino andando desde Guadalajara.*

During the original peopling of the Americas, the first inhabitants migrated across the Bering Straits and walked south across the continent. The oldest evidence of humankind in the U.S.—the Chicanos' ancient Indian ancestors—was found in Texas and has been dated to 35000 B.C.[3] In the Southwest United States archeologists have found 20,000-year-old campsites of the Indians who migrated through, or permanently occupied, the Southwest, Aztlán—the land of the herons, land of whiteness, the Edenic place of origin of the Azteca.

In 1000 B.C., descendants of the original Cochise people migrated into what is now Mexico and Central America and became the direct ancestors of many of the Mexican people. (The Cochise culture of the Southwest is the parent culture of the Aztecs. The Uto-Aztecan languages stemmed from the language of the Cochise people.)[4] The Aztecs (the Nahuatl word for people of Aztlán) left the Southwest in 1168 A.D.

Now let us go,
Tihueque, tihueque,
Vámonos, vámonos,
Un pájaro cantó.
Con sus ocho tribus salieron
de la "cueva del origen."
los aztecas siguieron al dios
Huitzilopochtli.

Huitzilopochtli, the God of War, guided them to the place (that later became Mexico City) where an eagle with a writhing serpent in its beak perched on a cactus. The eagle symbolizes the spirit (as the sun, the father); the serpent symbolizes the soul (as the earth, the mother). Together, they symbolize the struggle between the spiritual/celestial/male and the underworld/earth/ feminine. The symbolic sacrifice of the serpent to the "higher" masculine powers indicates that the patriarchal order had already vanquished the feminine and matriarchal order in pre-Columbian America.

At the beginning of the 16th century, the Spaniards and Hernán Cortés invaded Mexico and, with the help of the tribes that the Aztecs had subjugated, conquered it. Before the Conquest, there were twenty-five million Indian people in Mexico and the Yucatán. Immediately after the Conquest, the Indian population had been reduced to under seven million. By 1650, only one-and-a-half-million pure-blooded Indians remained. The *mestizos* who were genetically equipped to survive small pox, measles, and typhus (Old World diseases to which the natives had no immunity), founded a new hybrid race and inherited Central and South America.[5] *En 1521 nació una nueva raza, el mestizo, el mexicano* (people of mixed Indian and Spanish blood), a race that had never existed before. Chicanos, Mexican-Americans, are the offspring of those first matings.

Our Spanish, Indian, and *mestizo* ancestors explored and settled parts of the U.S. Southwest as early as the sixteenth century. For every gold-hungry *conquistador* and soul-hungry missionary who came north from Mexico, ten to twenty Indians and *mestizos* went along as porters or in other capacities.[6] For the Indians, this constituted a return to the place of origin, Aztlán, thus making Chicanos originally and secondarily indigenous to the Southwest. Indians and *mestizos* from central Mexico intermarried with North American Indians. The continual intermarriage between Mexican and American Indians and Spaniards formed an even greater *mestizaje*.

El destierro/The Lost Land

Entonces corré la sangre
no sabe el indio que hacer,
le van a quitar su tierra,
la tiene que defender,
el indio se cae muerto,   5
y el afuerino de pie.
Levántate, Manquilef.

Arauco tiene una pena
más negra que su chamal,
ya no son los españoles   10
los que les hacen llorar,
hoy son los propios chilenos
los que les quitan su pan.
Levántate, Pailahuan.
    —Violeta Parra, *"Arauco tiene una pena"*[7]

In the 1800s, Anglos migrated illegally into Texas, which was then part of Mexico, in greater and greater numbers and gradually drove the *tejanos* (native

Texans of Mexican descent) from their lands, committing all manner of atrocities against them. Their illegal invasion forced Mexico to fight a war to keep its Texas territory. The Battle of the Alamo, in which the Mexican forces vanquished the whites, became, for the whites, the symbol for the cowardly and villainous character of the Mexicans. It became (and still is) a symbol that legitimized the white imperialist takeover. With the capture of Santa Anna later in 1836, Texas became a republic. *Tejanos* lost their land and, overnight, became the foreigners.

Ya la mitad del terreno
les vendió el traidor Santa Anna,
con lo que se ha hecho muy rica
la nación americana.

¿Qué acaso no se conforman
con el oro de la minas?
Ustedes muy elegantes
y aquí nosotros en ruinas.
   —from the Mexican corrido, *"Del peligro de la Intervención"*[8]

In 1846, the U.S. incited Mexico to war. U.S. troops invaded and occupied Mexico, forcing her to give up almost half of her nation, what is now Texas, New Mexico, Arizona, Colorado and California.

With the victory of the U.S. forces over the Mexican in the U.S.-Mexican War, *los norteamericanos* pushed the Texas border down 100 miles, from *el río Nueces* to *el rió Grande*. South Texas ceased to be part of the Mexican state of Tamaulipas. Separated from Mexico, the Native Mexican-Texan no longer looked toward Mexico as home; the Southwest became our homeland once more. The border fence that divides the Mexican people was born on February 2, 1848 with the signing of the Treaty of Guadalupe-Hidalgo. It left 100,000 Mexican citizens on this side, annexed by conquest along with the land. The land established by the treaty as belonging to Mexicans was soon swindled away from its owners. The treaty was never honored and restitution, to this day, has never been made.

The justice and benevolence of God
will forbid that . . . Texas should again
become a howling wilderness
trod only by savages, or . . . benighted
by the ignorance and superstition,   5
the anarchy and rapine of Mexican misrule.
The Anglo-American race are destined
to be forever the proprietors of
this land of promise and fulfillment.
Their laws will govern it,   10
their learning will enlighten it,
their enterprise will improve it.
Their flocks range its boundless pastures,
for them its fertile lands will yield . . .
luxuriant harvests . . .   15

The wilderness of Texas has been redeemed
by Anglo-American blood & enterprise.
    —William H. Wharton[9]

The Gringo, locked into the fiction of white superiority, seized complete
political power, stripping Indians and Mexicans of their land while their feet
were still rooted in it. *Con el destierro y el exilo fuimos desuñados, destroncados,
destripados* — we were jerked out by the roots, truncated, disemboweled, dispos-
sessed, and separated from our identity and our history. Many, under the
threat of Anglo terrorism, abandoned homes and ranches and went to Mexico.
Some stayed and protested. But as the courts, law enforcement officials, and
government officials not only ignored their pleas but penalized them for their
efforts, *tejanos* had no other recourse but armed retaliation.

After Mexican-American resisters robbed a train in Brownsville, Texas on
October 8, 1915, Anglo vigilante groups began lynching Chicanos. Texas Rangers
would take them into the brush and shoot them. One hundred Chicanos were
killed in a matter of months, whole families lynched. Seven thousand fled to
Mexico, leaving their small ranches and farms. The Anglos, afraid that the *mexicanos*[10] would seek independence from the U.S., brought in 20,000 army
troops to put an end to the social protest movement in South Texas. Race
hatred had finally fomented into an all out war.[11]

My grandmother lost all her cattle,
they stole her land.

"Drought hit South Texas," my mother tells me. "*La tierra se puso bien seca y
los animales comenzaron a morrirse de se'. Mi papá se murió de un* heart attack
dejando a mamá pregnant *y con ocho huercos*, with eight kids and one on the way.
Yo fuí la mayor, tenía diez años. The next year the drought continued *y el ganado*
got hoof and mouth. *Se calleron* in droves *en las pastas el* brushland, *pansas blan-
cas* ballooning to the skies. *El siguiente año* still no rain. *Mi pobre madre viuda
perdió* two-thirds of her *ganado*. A smart *gabacho* lawyer took the land away *mamá*
hadn't paid taxes. *No hablaba inglés*, she didn't know how to ask for time to raise
the money." My father's mother, Mama Locha, also lost her *terreno*. For a while
we got $12.50 a year for the "mineral rights" of six acres of cemetery, all that was
left of the ancestral lands. Mama Locha had asked that we bury her there
beside her husband. *El cemeterio estaba cercado.* But there was a fence around the
cemetery, chained and padlocked by the ranch owners of the surrounding land.
We couldn't even get in to visit the graves, much less bury her there. Today, it is
still padlocked. The sign reads: "Keep out. Trespassers will be shot."

In the 1930s, after Anglo agribusiness corporations cheated the small Chicano landowners of their land, the corporations hired gangs of *mexicanos* to
pull out the brush, chaparral and cactus and to irrigate the desert. The land
they toiled over had once belonged to many of them, or had been used com-
munally by them. Later the Anglos brought in huge machines and root plows
and had the Mexicans scrape the land clean of natural vegetation. In my childhood I saw the end of dryland farming. I witnessed the land cleared; saw the
huge pipes connected to underwater sources sticking up in the air. As children,
we'd go fishing in some of those canals when they were full and hunt for
snakes in them when they were dry. In the 1950s I saw the land, cut up into

thousands of neat rectangles and squares, constantly being irrigated. In the 340-day growth season, the seeds of any kind of fruit or vegetable had only to be stuck in the ground in order to grow. More big land corporations came in and bought up the remaining land.

To make a living my father became a sharecropper. Rio Farms Incorporated loaned him seed money and living expenses. At harvest time, my father repaid the loan and forked over 40% of the earnings. Sometimes we earned less than we owed, but always the corporations fared well. Some had major holdings in vegetable trucking, livestock auctions and cotton gins. Altogether we lived on three successive Rio farms; the second was adjacent to the King Ranch and included a dairy farm; the third was a chicken farm. I remember the white feathers of three thousand Leghorn chickens blanketing the land for acres around. My sister, mother and I cleaned, weighed and packaged eggs. (For years afterwards I couldn't stomach the sight of an egg.) I remember my mother attending some of the meetings sponsored by well-meaning whites from Rio Farms. They talked about good nutrition, health, and held huge barbeques, The only thing salvaged for my family from those years are modern techniques of food canning and a food-stained book they printed made up of recipes from Rio Farms' Mexican women. How proud my mother was to have her recipe for *enchiladas coloradas* in a book.

El cruzar del mojado/Illegal Crossing

"Ahora si ya tengo una tumba para llorar,"
dice Conchita, upon being reunited with
her unknown mother just before the mother dies.
    —from Ismael Rodriguez' film, *Nosotros los pobres*[12]

    La crisis. Los gringos had not stopped at the border. By the end of the nineteenth century, powerful landowners in Mexico, in partnership with U.S. colonizing companies, had dispossessed millions of Indians of their lands. Currently, Mexico and her eighty million Citizens are almost completely dependent on the U.S. market. The Mexican government and wealthy growers are in partnership with such American conglomerates as American Motors, IT&T and Du Pont which own factories called *maquiladoras*. One-fourth of all Mexicans work at *maquiladoras*; most are young women. Next to oil, *maquiladoras* are Mexico's second greatest source of U.S. dollars. Working eight to twelve hours a day to wire in backup lights of U.S. autos or solder miniscule wires in TV sets is not the Mexican way. While the women are in the *maquiladoras*, the children are left on their own. Many roam the street, become part of *cholo* gangs. The infusion of the values of the white culture, coupled with the exploitation by that culture, is changing the Mexican way of life.
    The devaluation of the *peso* and Mexico's dependency on the U.S. have brought on what the Mexicans call *la crisis. No hay trabajo.* Half of the Mexican people are unemployed. In the U.S. a man or woman can make eight times what they can in Mexico. By March, 1987, 1,088 pesos were worth one U.S. dollar.* I remember when I was growing up in Texas how we'd cross the border at

*As this book goes to press, 13.2368 Mexican pesos are worth one U.S. dollar.

Reynosa or Progreso to buy sugar or medicines when the dollar was worth eight *pesos* and fifty *centavos*.

La travesía. For many *mexicanos del otro lado*, the choice is to stay in Mexico and starve or move north and live. *Dicen que cada mexicano siempre sueña de la conquista en los brazos de cuatro gringas rubias, la conquista del país poderoso del norte, los Estados Unidos. En cada Chicano y mexicano vive el mito del tesoro territorial perdido.* North Americans call this return to the homeland the silent invasion.

"A la cueva volverán"
— El Puma *en la cancion "Amalia"*

South of the border, called North America's rubbish dump by Chicanos, *mexicanos* congregate in the plazas to talk about the best way to cross. Smugglers, *coyotes, pasadores, enganchadores* approach these people or are sought out by them. *"¿Qué dicen muchachos a echársela de mojado?"*

"Now among the alien gods with
weapons of magic am I."
— Navajo protection song, sung when going into battle.[13]

We have a tradition of migration, a tradition of long walks. Today we are witnessing *la migración de los pueblos mexicanos*, the return odyssey to the historical/mythological Aztlán. This time, the traffic is from south to north.

El retorno to the promised land first began with the Indians from the interior of Mexico and the *mestizos* that came with the *conquistadores* in the 1500s. Immigration continued in the next three centuries, and, in this century, it continued with the *braceros* who helped to build our railroads and who picked our fruit. Today thousands of Mexicans are crossing the border legally and illegally; ten million people without documents have returned to the Southwest.

Faceless, nameless, invisible, taunted with "Hey cucaracho" (cockroach). Trembling with fear, yet filled with courage, a courage born of desperation. Barefoot and uneducated, Mexicans with hands like boot soles gather at night by the river where two worlds merge creating what Reagan* calls a frontline, a war zone. The convergence has created a shock culture, a border culture, a third country, a closed country.

Without benefit of bridges, the *"mojados"* (wetbacks) float on inflatable rafts across *el río Grande*, or wade or swim across naked, clutching their clothes over their heads. Holding onto the grass, they pull themselves along the banks with a prayer to *Virgen de Guadalupe* on their lips: *Ay virgencita morena, mi madrecita, dame tu bendición.*

The Border Patrol hides behind the local McDonalds on the outskirts of Brownsville, Texas or some other border town. They set traps around the river beds beneath the bridge.[14] Hunters in army-green uniforms stalk and track these economic refugees by the powerful nightvision of electronic sensing devices planted in the ground or mounted on Border Patrol vans. Cornered by flashlights, frisked while their arms stretch over their heads, *los mojados* are handcuffed, locked in jeeps, and then kicked back across the border.

*When Anzaldúa wrote this essay, Ronald Reagan (1911–2004) was the president of the United States. He served two terms, from 1981 to 1989.

One out of every three is caught. Some return to enact their rite of passage as many as three times a day. Some of those who make it across undetected fall prey to Mexican robbers such as those in Smugglers' Canyon on the American side of the border near Tijuana. As refugees in a homeland that does not want them, many find a welcome hand holding out only suffering, pain, and ignoble death.

Those who make it past the checking points of the Border Patrol find themselves in the midst of 150 years of racism in Chicano *barrios* in the Southwest and in big northern cities. Living in a no-man's-borderland, caught between being treated as criminals and being able to eat, between resistance and deportation, the illegal refugees are some of the poorest and the most exploited of any people in the U.S. It is illegal for Mexicans to work without green cards. But big farming combines, farm bosses and smugglers who bring them in make money off the "wetbacks'" labor — they don't have to pay federal minimum wages, or ensure adequate housing or sanitary conditions.

The Mexican woman is especially at risk. Often the *coyote* (smuggler) doesn't feed her for days or let her go to the bathroom. Often he rapes her or sells her into prostitution. She cannot call on county or state health or economic resources because she doesn't know English and she fears deportation. American employers are quick to take advantage of her helplessness. She can't go home. She's sold her house, her furniture, borrowed from friends in order to pay the *coyote* who charges her four or five thousand dollars to smuggle her to Chicago. She may work as a live-in maid for white, Chicano or Latino households for as little as $15 a week. Or work in the garment industry, do hotel work. Isolated and worried about her family back home, afraid of getting caught and deported, living with as many as fifteen people in one room, the *mexicana* suffers serious health problems. *Se enferma de los nervios, de alta presión.*[15]

La mojada, la mujer indocumentada, is doubly threatened in this country. Not only does she have to contend with sexual violence, but like all women, she is prey to a sense of physical helplessness. As a refugee, she leaves the familiar and safe homeground to venture into unknown and possibly dangerous terrain.

This is her home
       this thin edge of
          barbwire.

NOTES

1. Los Tigres del Norte is a *conjunto* band.
2. Jack D. Forbes, *Aztecas del Norte: The Chicanos of Aztlán* (Greenwich, CT: Fawcett Publications, Premier Books, 1973), 13, 183; Eric R. Wolf, *Sons of Shaking Earth* (Chicago, IL: University of Chicago Press, Phoenix Books, 1959), 32.
3. John R. Chávez, *The Lost Land: The Chicano Images of the Southwest* (Albuquerque, NM: University of New Mexico Press, 1984), 9.
4. Chávez, 9. Besides the Aztecs, the Ute, Gabrillino of California, Pima of Arizona, some Pueblo of New Mexico, Comanche of Texas, Opata of Sonora, Tarahumara of Sinaloa and Durango, and the Huichol of Jalisco speak Uto-Aztecan languages and are descended from the Cochise people.
5. Reay Tannahill, *Sex in History* (Briarcliff Manor, NY: Stein and Day Publishers/Scarborough House, 1980), 308.
6. Chávez, 21.
7. Isabel Parra, *El Libro Major de Violeta Parra* (Madrid, España: Ediciones Michay, S.A., 1985), 156–7.

8. From the Mexican *corrido, "Del peligro de la Intervención."* Vicente T. Mendoza, *El Corrido Mexicano* (México, D.F.: Fonda De Cultura Económica, 1954), 42.

9. Arnoldo De León, *They Called Them Greasers: Anglo Attitudes Toward Mexicans in Texas, 1821–1900* (Austin, TX: University of Texas Press, 1983), 2–3.

10. The Plan of San Diego, Texas, drawn up on January 6, 1915, called for the independence and segregation of the states bordering Mexico: Texas, New Mexico, Arizona, Colorado, and California. Indians would get their land back. Blacks would get six states from the south and form their own independent republic. Chávez, 79.

11. Jesús Mena, "Violence in the Rio Grande Valley," *Nuestro* (Jan/Feb. 1983), 41–42.

12. *Nosotros los pobres* was the first Mexican film that was truly Mexican and not an imitation European film. It stressed the devotion and love that children should have for their mother and how its lack would lead to the dissipation of their character. This film spawned a generation of mother-devotion/ungrateful-sons films.

13. From the Navajo "Protection Song" (to be sung upon going into battle). George W. Gronyn, ed., *American Indian Poetry: The Standard Anthology of Songs and Chants* (New York, NY: Liveright, 1934), 97.

14. Grace Halsell, *Los ilegales*, trans. Mayo Antonio Sánchez (Editorial Diana Mexica, 1979).

15. Margarita B. Melville, "Mexican Women Adapt to Migration," *International Migration Review*, 1978.

QUESTIONS FOR CRITICAL THINKING AND WRITING

1. In the poem that opens her essay, why does Anzaldúa state the border fence is useless? Do you agree? Why or why not?

2. When was the border fence put into place? What immediate effect did it have?

3. Why, according to Anzaldúa, is the Mexican woman returning to Aztlán particularly at risk? Why do you think she places herself in such danger in order to make the journey and live there?

4. **RESEARCH AND WRITE.** Toward the end of her essay, Anzaldúa summarizes the experience of Mexicans living in their own country who are in many ways dependent upon or subjugated by the United States. Research the problem she describes as *la crisis*. In a brief essay, compare what you have learned with Anzaldúa's description of the situation.

RICK BASS

© Nicole Blaisdell.

Rick Bass was born in Fort Worth, Texas, in 1958. His first book of short stories was called *The Watch*. Set in Texas, it won the PEN/ Nelson Algren Award. A winner also of the Pushcart Prize and O. Henry Award, Bass has written more than twenty books of fiction and nonfiction. These works include *The Lives of Rocks*, from which the following story comes; *Where the Sea Used to Be*; *The Diezmo*; *The Deer Pasture*; *Colter: The True Story of the Best Dog I Ever Had*; *The Roadless Yaak: Reflections and Observations About One of Our Last Great Wilderness Areas*; and *Caribou Rising: Defending the Porcupine*

Herd, Gwich-'in Culture, and the Arctic National Wildlife Refuge. In *Bloomsbury Review,* John Murray wrote that "Bass is characteristically Southwestern in independence, his restlessness, his humor, his vitality, his sunny outlook, his distrust of unchallenged authority, and his disclaim for affectation and pretense."

BEFORE YOU READ

Rick Bass, a writer and an environmental activist, often gives nature and the elements the same weight as human characters in his stories. In the following story, how does the physical world appear to take on a life of its own? What is the relationship between nature and human emotion in the story?

The Windy Day   2006

The last day of my life before I knew what I would be the father of—a son or a daughter—was a good one. It was in October, the fourth month, and there'd been high winds flapping the tin on our cabin roof all through the night. We woke up thinking, *This is the day we drive to town and find out.*

That morning there was smoke all through the valley, an eerie green fog, and the taste of smoke was everywhere, and ash was falling from the sky like snow.

We sat around in that strange green light that we had never seen before and waited until it was time to leave for town. The wind was gusting to sixty and then seventy miles an hour. We could hear trees crashing in the forest. I knew there'd be some trees down across the road, but I had no idea how many.

"Maybe we should wait," Elizabeth said.

I think she meant wait another month, or even the remaining five months.

But I was ready. I had waited thirty-three years already. Waiting's fine up to a point. I was ready. I was pretty sure I was ready.

The tops of trees were blowing through the sky. The forest was being rent apart, tunnels of wind snapping their way through the great forever larch trees, breaking them off up high, where the winds were gustier: seventy, eighty, ninety miles an hour.

Ash was rushing everywhere.

I loaded the chain saw, extra gas and oil, and wrenches into the back of the truck; loaded up an overshirt and my heavy leather gloves. It would be okay to show up at the hospital with just a little bit of gasoline and wood chips on me. It was Elizabeth who was going to get tested—ultrasounded—not me. I was just going to stand there and hold her hand, and watch the screen.

Deer and moose were running through the woods, not knowing, as we did, that the fire was still fifteen miles away, that it was still safe, just smoky.

And windy.

I had to stop and cut a tree about every hundred yards or so in the first mile. But that was okay. It was exciting—all those branches and boughs floating past, some of them caught in dust-devil swirls high over our heads. It was midday, but growing so dark from the ash and smoke that we had our headlights on—almost as dark as night, but in that strange *green* way. Sometimes the vague light would grow so suddenly dim that it was as if someone were dimming it on purpose, the glow fading almost away and the blackness coming on, night in the middle of the day. But then it would turn green again, the dullest light, and I would make two neat cuts in each tree and roll the log off to the side of the road and pass through, on to the next tree.

"We have to be careful," Elizabeth shouted as the trees fell all around us.

"Do you want to go back?" I asked once.

"No," she said.

We watched ahead of us, and to the side, to be careful not to be pinned by any falling trees. The wind was so strong and indecisive that you couldn't tell which way the trees were going to fall until they snapped. Sometimes we'd see them fall in the woods; other times we'd see them fall across the road just in front of us and farther on up the road. The trees were falling behind us, too, closing off our return, but that didn't matter.

It was twelve miles out to the main road, and after that I hoped it would get better. The road was a little wider out there, and maybe someone with a chain saw would have already gone through ahead of us.

I moved slowly but steadily. There wasn't any rush. I liked cutting the fallen trees and moving them to one side. Carrying my wife and child — *child* — through the storm. I didn't think of the trees as being dangerous or my enemy. I had to be careful and look up when I was cutting because I couldn't hear the snap and crack and splinter when the saw was running. Elizabeth, in the truck, had to look up and all around and make sure nothing fell on top of the truck while she was in it. I tried to park it next to ridges or high banks so that a falling tree would land against the road bank rather than crashing all the way down onto the truck.

I had not wanted to know, and had not wanted to know, but then I suddenly wanted to know. It was just a windy day. Maybe a little too windy. But it is so hard to turn back. Some of the trees were so big. Gold-needled larch boughs carpeted the narrow road, branches upturned like torn arms. The woods smelled heavily of smoke but also of fresh sap. It was a crisp, heady smell that made me want to keep cutting all the way to Libby, more than forty miles away. Which was where we were going. We hadn't yet realized there would be even more trees down across the main road.

We got to the main road about an hour before dark. We'd long since missed our appointment. But I didn't care, I was revved up, had long ago fallen into the mood of the crashing forest — cut cut roll, drive on, cut cut roll, drive on. Treetops were still hurtling past us as if in a hurricane, and that dense green smoky light was pulsing and darkening, dimming and glimmering, and giving way to true dark.

"Let's go back," Elizabeth said finally. We still had nearly forty miles to go. "We can try again tomorrow," she said.

I didn't want to go back. It seemed an impossibility for me to go back. We had cut our way out to the main road. I still had the saw in my hands and plenty of gas left. It was dark. But I still had that saw in my hands.

"Okay," I said.

Though if it was a girl, in sixteen years the two of us would be riding horses through these very woods, leaping some of the rotting logs that had fallen this day, riding through sweet fir-scented woods in the autumn on fine muscular horses whose bellies creaked and who farted wildly with each jump, each lift and gather over the fallen logs; and if it was a boy, in sixteen years we would be pulling logs out of the woods, fastening cables to them and pulling them through the woods with those very same horses, in that same autumn, to repair the buck-and-rail fence that another wind had disrupted.

I still had the saw in my hands.

"Okay," I said, branches and limbs floating and drifting through the thick ashy air like streamers and kites, pieces of trees rising and falling on all the hot, smoky, crazy currents, trees swaying from side to side, popping and snapping, and Elizabeth and me guarding what we had, what we were taking with us, out of the woods and into the future, watching all around us for those devil falling snags, those crashing trees; and me with the saw, inching our way through the wreckage, the fresh sweet smell of sap and crushed boughs, cutting our thin lane straight through the forest to the light.

QUESTIONS FOR CRITICAL THINKING AND WRITING

1. Why do you think the characters in this story continue to go forward even though they have missed their appointment?
2. Is it important to the narrator if his child is a boy or a girl? Why or why not?
3. If the story reflects the experience these characters are about to have as new parents, do you think it reflects it truthfully? How so?
4. In stories, conflict tends to motivate characters or shape the action of the plot. What is the conflict of "The Windy Day"? In a few succinct paragraphs, explain which forces oppose each other in the story and how conflict affects what happens. Does the story come to a satisfactory conclusion? Is the conflict resolved?

CHIEF TEN BEARS

Chief Ten Bears, whose Comanche name was Paruasemana, was born in 1790 and died in 1872. The Lakota Indians killed off members of his family when he was an infant, leaving him orphaned. In 1863, he visited Washington on behalf of the Comanches, and in 1867, he took part in a meeting at Medicine Lodge Creek, near Medicine Lodge, Barber County, Kansas, in an effort to create a lasting peace treaty between the U.S. federal government and the southern Indian tribes. The speech that follows reflects Ten Bears's attempt to give the Comanches' perspective on the influx of settlers into Indian lands. "If the Texans had kept out of my country," he said, "there might have been peace." In his words, the Comanches hoped the Texans would respect their one desire to "wander on the prairie until [they] die" instead of placing them on reservations.

BEFORE YOU READ

In the following speech, Chief Ten Bears addresses the men who claim that Native Americans are violating the white man's treaties. Why do you think there were problems with treaties between the Indians and the whites? What do you think the Native Americans found objectionable about such treaties?

Chief Ten Bears.
Courtesy, National Museum of the American Indian, Smithsonian Institution (P00576). Photo by
William Henry Jackson.

Speech Setting Forth the Case of the Comanches, October 20, 1867

The Federal government in 1865 made the unsatisfactory Treaty of the Little Arkansas with the Comanche and Kiowa Indians. By the summer of 1866 the Indians were violating it, as a government investigating commission later confirmed. Congress then in June, 1867, authorized a peace commission to correct the causes of the Indian complaints and to secure a lasting peace. The commissioners met the Indians at Medicine Lodge Creek, near the present site of Medicine Lodge, Barber County, Kansas, and on October 21, 1867, signed a treaty of peace with the southern tribes. It was the last ever made with the Comanches, Cheyennes, Arapahos, Kiowas, and Kiowa-Apaches, and was the occasion of one of the last old-fashioned Indian gatherings. When the council opened, the Indians were told that they had been violating the treaties and were urged to state their side of the case. Ten Bears of the Yep-eaters (the most northern Comanche band) spoke for the Comanches on October 20. Having seen the numbers of the white man, as well as his wealth and power, on his visit to Washington two years before, he realized that the proposals represented an alternative between refuge on the white man's terms or utter destruction, but he pleaded the Comanche case. His presentation is a masterpiece of logic and oratory.

—From Documents of Texas History, *edited by Ernest Wallace et al.*

My heart is filled with joy when I see you here, as the brooks fill with water when the snows melt in the spring; and I feel glad as the ponies do when the fresh grass starts in the beginning of the year. I heard of your coming when I was many sleeps away, and I made but few camps before I met you. I knew that you had come to do good to me and to my people. I looked for benefits which would last forever, and so my face shines with joy as I look upon you. My people have never first drawn a bow or fired a gun against the whites. There has been trouble on the line between us, and my young men have danced the war dance. But it was not begun by us. It was you who sent out the first soldier and we who sent out the second. Two years ago, I came upon this road, following the buffalo, that my wives and children might have their cheeks plump and their bodies warm. But the soldiers fired on us, and since that time there has been a noise like that of a thunderstorm, and we have not known which way to go. So it was upon the Canadian. Nor have we been made to cry once alone. The blue-dressed soldiers and the Utes came from out of the night when it was dark and still, and for camp-fires they lit our lodges. Instead of hunting game they killed my braves, and the warriors of the tribe cut short their hair for the dead.

So it was in Texas. They made sorrow come in our camps, and we went out like the buffalo bulls when the cows are attacked. When we found them we killed them, and their scalps hang in our lodges. The Comanches are not weak and blind, like the pups of a dog when seven sleeps old. They are strong and far-sighted, like grown horses. We took their road and we went on it. The white women cried and our women laughed.

But there are things which you have said to me which I do not like. They were not sweet like sugar, but bitter like gourds. You said that you wanted to put us upon a reservation, to build us houses and make us medicine lodges. I do not want them. I was born upon the prairie, where the wind blew free and there was nothing to break the light of the sun. I was born where there were no enclosures and everything drew a free breath. I want to die there and not within walls. I know every stream and every wood between the Rio Grande and the Arkansas. I have hunted and lived over that country. I live like my fathers before me and like them I lived happily.

When I was at Washington the Great Father told me that all the Comanche land was ours, and that no one should hinder us in living upon it. So, why do you ask us to leave the rivers, and the sun, and the wind, and live in houses? Do not speak of it more. I love to carry out the talk I get from the Great Father. When I get goods and presents, I and my people feel glad, since it shows that he holds us in his eye.

If the Texans had kept out of my country, there might have been peace. But that which you now say we must live in, is too small. The Texans have taken away the places where the grass grew the thickest and the timber was the best. Had we kept that, we might have done the things you ask. But it is too late. The whites have the country which we loved, and we only wish to wander on the prairie until we die. Any good thing you say to me shall not be forgotten. I shall carry it as near to my heart as my children, and it shall be as often on my tongue as the name of the Great Spirit. I want no blood upon my land to stain the grass. I want it all clear and pure, and I wish it so that all who go through among my people may find peace when they come in and leave it when they go out.

QUESTIONS FOR CRITICAL THINKING AND WRITING

1. How does Chief Ten Bears feel about the white colonists?

2. What understanding did Chief Ten Bears share with the "Great Father"? What is being asked of him now, as he delivers this speech, that contradicts this understanding?

3. According to Chief Ten Bears, what happened between the Native Americans and the white soldiers in Texas?

4. In a few paragraphs, discuss Chief Ten Bears's approach to his audience in his speech. How does it begin? What is his argument? How does he support his argument? How does he conclude? Overall, how persuasive is his speech? Explain.

SANDRA CISNEROS

Sandra Cisneros was born in 1954 to a family that included six brothers. She spent much of her life moving between Mexico and Chicago. She earned a BA in English from Loyola University of Chicago and an MFA in creative writing from the Iowa Writers' Workshop. Her books include *Woman Hollering Creek and Other Stories*, from which the following story comes, *My Wicked Wicked Ways*, *Caramelo*, and a collection of poems titled *Loose Woman*; she is best known for her novel *The House on Mango Street*. Her Mexican heritage figures prominently in many of her works of fiction, and she combines Spanish and English freely in her writing. On the mixing of Spanish into her work, Cisneros has said: "All of a sudden something happens to the English, something really new is happening, a new spice is added to the English language." She currently lives in San Antonio, Texas.

BEFORE YOU READ

"Woman Hollering Creek" follows the character Cleófilas, who as a young bride moves from Mexico to Texas. What do Cleófilas and Woman Hollering Creek have in common? How and why does the protagonist finally take control of her life?

Woman Hollering Creek   *1991*

The day Don Serafín gave Juan Pedro Martínez Sánchez permission to take Cleófilas Enriqueta DeLeón Hernández as his bride, across her father's threshold, over several miles of dirt road and several miles of paved, over one border and beyond to a town *en el otro lado* — on the other side — already did he divine the morning his daughter would raise her hand over her eyes, look south, and dream of returning to the chores that never ended, six good-for-nothing brothers, and one old man's complaints.

He had said, after all, in the hubbub of parting: I am your father, I will never abandon you. He *had* said that, hadn't he, when he hugged and then let her go. But at the moment Cleófilas was busy looking for Chela, her maid of honor, to fulfill their bouquet conspiracy. She would not remember her father's parting words until later. *I am your father, I will never abandon you.*

Only now as a mother did she remember. Now, when she and Juan Pedrito sat by the creek's edge. How when a man and a woman love each other, sometimes that love sours. But a parent's love for a child, a child's for its parents, is another thing entirely.

This is what Cleófilas thought evenings when Juan Pedro did not come home, and she lay on her side of the bed listening to the hollow roar of the interstate, a distant dog barking, the pecan trees rustling like ladies in stiff petticoats — *shh-shh-shh, shh-shh-shh* — soothing her to sleep.

In the town where she grew up, there isn't very much to do except accompany the aunts and godmothers to the house of one or the other to play cards. Or walk to the cinema to see this week's film again, speckled and with one hair quivering annoyingly on the screen. Or to the center of town to order a milk shake that will appear in a day and a half as a pimple on her backside. Or to the girlfriend's house to watch the latest *telenovela* episode and try to copy the way the women comb their hair, wear their makeup.

But what Cleófilas has been waiting for, has been whispering and sighing and giggling for, has been anticipating since she was old enough to lean against the window displays of gauze and butterflies and lace, is passion. Not the kind on the cover of the *¡Alarma!* magazines, mind you, where the lover is photographed with the bloody fork she used to salvage her good name. But passion in its purest crystalline essence. The kind the books and songs and *telenovelas* describe when one finds, finally, the great love of one's life, and does whatever one can, must do, at whatever the cost.

Tú o Nadie. "You or No One." The title of the current favorite *telenovela*. The beautiful Lucía Méndez having to put up with all kinds of hardships of the heart, separation and betrayal, and loving, always loving no matter what, because *that* is the most important thing, and did you see Lucía Méndez on the Bayer aspirin commercials — wasn't she lovely? Does she dye her hair do you think? Cleófilas is going to go to the *farmacía* and buy a hair rinse; her girlfriend Chela will apply it — it's not that difficult at all.

Because you didn't watch last night's episode when Lucía confessed she loved him more than anyone in her life. In her life! And she sings the song "You or No One" in the beginning and end of the show. *Tú o Nadie.* Somehow one ought to live one's life like that, don't you think? You or no one. Because to suffer for love is good. The pain all sweet somehow. In the end.

Seguín. She had liked the sound of it. Far away and lovely. Not like *Monclova. Coahuia.* Ugly.

Seguín, Tejas. A nice sterling ring to it. The tinkle of money. She would get to wear outfits like the women on the *tele*, like Lucía Méndez. And have a lovely house, and wouldn't Chela be jealous.

And yes, they will drive all the way to Laredo to get her wedding dress. That's what they say. Because Juan Pedro wants to get married right away, without a long engagement since he can't take off too much time from work. He has a very important position in Seguín with, with . . . a beer company, I think. Or was it tires? Yes, he has to be back. So they will get married in the spring when he can take off work, and then they will drive off in his new pickup—did you see it?—to their new home in Seguín. Well, not exactly new, but they're going to repaint the house. You know newlyweds. New paint and new furniture. Why not? He can afford it. And later on add maybe a room or two for the children. May they be blessed with many.

Well, you'll see. Cleófilas has always been so good with her sewing machine. A little *rrrr, rrrr, rrrr* of the machine and *¡zas!* Miracles. She's always been so clever, that girl. Poor thing. And without even a mama to advise her on things like her wedding night. Well, may God help her. What with a father with a head like a burro, and those six clumsy brothers. Well, what do you think! Yes, I'm going to the wedding. Of course! The dress I want to wear just needs to be altered a teensy bit to bring it up to date. See, I saw a new style last night that I thought would suit me. Did you watch last night's episode of *The Rich Also Cry*? Well, did you notice the dress the mother was wearing?

La Gritona. Such a funny name for such a lovely *arroyo*. But that's what they called the creek that ran behind the house. Though no one could say whether the woman had hollered from anger or pain. The natives only knew the *arroyo* one crossed on the way to San Antonio, and then once again on the way back, was called Woman Hollering, a name no one from these parts questioned, little less understood. *Pues, allá de los indios, quién sabe*—who knows, the townspeople shrugged, because it was of no concern to their lives how this trickle of water received its curious name.

"What do you want to know for?" Trini the laundromat attendant asked in the same gruff Spanish she always used whenever she gave Cleófilas change or yelled at her for something. First for putting too much soap in the machines. Later, for sitting on a washer. And still later, after Juan Pedrito was born, for not understanding that in this country you cannot let your baby walk around with no diaper and his pee-pee hanging out, it wasn't nice, *¿entiendes? Pues.*

How could Cleófilas explain to a woman like this why the name Woman Hollering fascinated her. Well, there was no sense talking to Trini.

On the other hand there were the neighbor ladies, one on either side of the house they rented near the *arroyo*. The woman Soledad on the left, the woman Dolores on the right.

The neighbor lady Soledad liked to call herself a widow, though how she came to be one was a mystery. Her husband had either died, or run away with an ice-house floozie, or simply gone out for cigarettes one afternoon and never came back. It was hard to say which since Soledad, as a rule, didn't mention him.

In the other house lived *la señora* Dolores, kind and very sweet, but her house smelled too much of incense and candles from the altars that burned continuously in memory of two sons who had died in the last war and one husband who had died shortly after from grief. The neighbor lady Dolores divided her time between the memory of these men and her garden, famous for its sunflowers—so tall they had to be supported with broom handles and old boards; red red cockscombs, fringed and bleeding a thick menstrual color; and, especially, roses whose sad scent reminded Cleófilas of the dead. Each Sunday *la señora* Dolores clipped the most beautiful of these flowers and arranged them on three modest headstones at the Seguin cemetery.

The neighbor ladies, Soledad, Dolores, they might've known once the name of the *arroyo* before it turned English but they did not know now. They were too busy remembering the men who had left through either choice or circumstance and would never come back.

Pain or rage, Cleófilas wondered when she drove over the bridge the first time as a newlywed and Juan Pedro had pointed it out. *La Gritona*, he had said, and she had laughed. Such a funny name for a creek so pretty and full of happily ever after.

The first time she had been so surprised she didn't cry out or try to defend herself. She had always said she would strike back if a man, any man, were to strike her.

But when the moment came, and he slapped her once, and then again, and again, until the lip split and bled an orchid of blood, she didn't fight back, she didn't break into tears, she didn't run away as she imagined she might when she saw such things in the *telenovelas*.

In her own home her parents had never raised a hand to each other or to their children. Although she admitted she may have been brought up a little leniently as an only daughter — *la consentida*, the princess — there were some things she would never tolerate. Ever.

Instead, when it happened the first time, when they were barely man and wife, she had been so stunned, it left her speechless, motionless, numb. She had done nothing but reach up to the heat on her mouth and stare at the blood on her hand as if even then she didn't understand.

She could think of nothing to say, said nothing. Just stroked the dark curls of the man who wept and would weep like a child, his tears of repentance and shame, this time and each.

The men at the ice house. From what she can tell, from the times during her first year when still a newlywed she is invited and accompanies her husband, sits mute beside their conversation, waits and sips a beer until it grows warm, twists a paper napkin into a knot, then another into a fan, one into a rose, nods her head, smiles, yawns, politely grins, laughs at the appropriate moments, leans against her husband's sleeve, tugs at his elbow, and finally becomes good at predicting where the talk will lead, from this Cleófilas concludes each is nightly trying to find the truth lying at the bottom of the bottle like a gold doubloon on the sea floor.

They want to tell each other what they want to tell themselves. But what is bumping like a helium balloon at the ceiling of the brain never finds its way out. It bubbles and rises, it gurgles in the throat, it rolls across the surface of the tongue, and erupts from the lips — a belch.

If they are lucky, there are tears at the end of the long night. At any given moment, the fists try to speak. They are dogs chasing their own tails before lying down to sleep, trying to find a way, a route, an out, and — finally — get some peace.

In the morning sometimes before he opens his eyes. Or after they have finished loving. Or at times when he is simply across from her at the table putting pieces of food into his mouth and chewing. Cleófilas thinks, This is the man I have waited my whole life for.

Not that he isn't a good man. She has to remind herself why she loves him when she changes the baby's Pampers, or when she mops the bathroom floor, or tries to make the curtains for the doorways without doors, or whiten the linen. Or wonder a little when he kicks the refrigerator and says he hates this shitty house and is going out where he won't be bothered with the baby's howling and her suspicious questions, and her requests to fix this and this and this because if she had any brains in her head she'd realize he's been up before the rooster earning his living to pay for the food in her belly and the roof over her head and would have to wake up again early the next day so why can't you just leave me in peace, woman.

He is not very tall, no, and he doesn't look like the men on the *telenovelas*. His face still scarred from acne. And he has a bit of a belly from all the beer he drinks. Well, he's always been husky.

This man who fans and belches and snores as well as laughs and kisses and holds her. Somehow this husband whose whiskers she finds each morning in the sink, whose shoes she must air each evening on the porch, this husband who cuts his fingernails in public, laughs loudly, curses like a man, and demands each course of dinner be served on a separate plate like at his mother's, as soon as he gets home, on time or late, and who doesn't care at all for music or *telenovelas* or romance or roses or the moon floating pearly over the *arroyo*, or through the bedroom window for that matter, shut the blinds and go back to sleep, this man, this father, this rival, this keeper, this lord, this master, this husband till kingdom come.

A doubt. Slender as a hair. A washed cup set back on the shelf wrong-side-up. Her lipstick, and body talc, and hairbrush all arranged in the bathroom a different way.

No. Her imagination. The house the same as always. Nothing.

Coming home from the hospital with her new son, her husband. Something comforting in discovering her house slippers beneath the bed, the faded housecoat where she left it on the bathroom hook. Her pillow. Their bed.

Sweet sweet homecoming. Sweet as the scent of face powder in the air, jasmine, sticky liquor.

Smudged fingerprint on the door. Crushed cigarette in a glass. Wrinkle in the brain crumpling to a crease.

Sometimes she thinks of her father's house. But how could she go back there? What a disgrace. What would the neighbors say? Coming home like that with one baby on her hip and one in the oven. Where's your husband?

The town of gossips. The town of dust and despair. Which she has traded for this town of gossips. This town of dust, despair. Houses farther apart perhaps, though no more privacy because of it. No leafy *zócalo* in the center of the town, though the murmur of talk is clear enough all the same. No huddled whispering on the church steps each Sunday. Because here the whispering begins at sunset at the ice house instead.

This town with its silly pride for a bronze pecan the size of a baby carriage in front of the city hall. TV repair shop, drugstore, hardware, dry cleaner's, chiropractor's, liquor store, bail bonds, empty storefront, and nothing, nothing, nothing of interest. Nothing one could walk to, at any rate. Because the towns here are built so that you have to depend on husbands. Or you stay home. Or you drive. If you're rich enough to own, allowed to drive, your own car.

There is no place to go. Unless one counts the neighbor ladies. Soledad on one side, Dolores on the other. Or the creek.

Don't go out there after dark, *mi'jita*. Stay near the house. *No es bueno para la salud. Mala suerte.* Bad luck. *Mal aire.* You'll get sick and the baby too. You'll catch a fright wandering about in the dark, and then you'll see how right we were.

The stream sometimes only a muddy puddle in the summer, though now in the springtime, because of the rains, a good-size alive thing, a thing with a voice all its own, all day and all night calling in its high, silver voice. Is it La Llorona, the weeping woman? La Llorona, who drowned her own children. Perhaps La Llorona is the one they named the creek after, she thinks, remembering all the stories she learned as a child.

La Llorona calling to her. She is sure of it. Cleófilas sets the baby's Donald Duck blanket on the grass. Listens. The day sky turning to night. The baby pulling up fistfuls of grass and laughing. La Llorona. Wonders if something as quiet as this drives a woman to the darkness under the trees.

What she needs is . . . and made a gesture as if to yank a woman's buttocks to his groin. Maximiliano, the foul-smelling fool from across the road, said this and set the men laughing, but Cleófilas just muttered, *Grosera*, and went on washing dishes.

She knew he said it not because it was true, but more because it was he who needed to sleep with a woman, instead of drinking each night at the ice house and stumbling home alone.

Maximiliano who was said to have killed his wife in an ice-house brawl when she came at him with a mop. I had to shoot, he had said — she was armed.

Their laughter outside the kitchen window. Her husband's, his friends'. Manolo, Beto, Efraín, el Perico. Maximiliano.

Was Cleófilas just exaggerating as her husband always said? It seemed the newspapers were full of such stories. This woman found on the side of the interstate. This one pushed from a moving car. This one's cadaver, this one unconscious, this one beaten blue. Her ex-husband, her husband, her lover, her father, her brother, her uncle, her friend, her co-worker. Always. The same grisly news in the pages of the dailies. She dunked a glass under the soapy water for a moment — shivered.

He had thrown a book. Hers. From across the room. A hot welt across the cheek. She could forgive that. But what stung more was the fact it was *her* book, a love story by Corín Tellado, what she loved most now that she lived in the U.S., without a television set, without the *telenovelas*.

Except now and again when her husband was away and she could manage it, the few episodes glimpsed at the neighbor lady Soledad's house because Dolores didn't care for that sort of thing, though Soledad was often kind enough to retell what had happened on what episode of *María de Nadie*, the poor Argentine country girl who had the ill fortune of falling in love with the beautiful son of the Arrocha family, the very family she worked for, whose roof she slept under and whose floors she vacuumed, while in that same house, with the dust brooms and floor cleaners as witnesses, the square-jawed Juan Carlos Arrocha had uttered words of love, I love you, María, listen to me, *mi querida*, but it was she who had to say No, no, we are not of the same class, and remind him it was not his place nor hers to fall in love, while all the while her heart was breaking, can you imagine.

Cleófilas thought her life would have to be like that, like a *telenovela*, only now the episodes got sadder and sadder. And there were no commercials in between for comic relief. And no happy ending in sight. She thought this when she sat with the baby out by the creek behind the house. Cleófilas de . . . ? But somehow she would have to change her name to Topazio, or Yesenia, Cristal, Adriana, Stefania, Andrea, something more poetic than Cleófilas. Everything happened to women with names like jewels. But what happened to a Cleófilas? Nothing. But a crack in the face.

Because the doctor has said so. She has to go. To make sure the new baby is all right, so there won't be any problems when he's born, and the appointment card says next Tuesday. Could he please take her. And that's all.

No, she won't mention it. She promises. If the doctor asks she can say she fell down the front steps or slipped when she was out in the backyard, slipped out back, she could tell him that. She has to go back next Tuesday, Juan Pedro, please, for the new baby. For their child.

She could write to her father and ask maybe for money, just a loan, for the new baby's medical expenses. Well then if he'd rather she didn't. All right, she won't. Please don't anymore. Please don't. She knows it's difficult saving money with all the bills they have, but how else are they going to get out of debt with the truck payments? And after the rent and the food and the electricity and the gas and the water and the who-knows-what, well, there's hardly anything left. But please, at least for the doctor visit. She won't ask for anything else. She has to. Why is she so anxious? Because.

Because she is going to make sure the baby is not turned around backward this time to split her down the center. Yes. Next Tuesday at five-thirty. I'll have Juan Pedrito dressed and ready. But those are the only shoes he has. I'll polish them, and we'll be ready. As soon as you come from work. We won't make you ashamed.

Felice? It's me, Graciela.

No, I can't talk louder. I'm at work.

Look, I need kind of a favor. There's a patient, a lady here who's got a problem.

Well, wait a minute. Are you listening to me or what?

I can't talk real loud 'cause her husband's in the next room.

Well, would you just listen?

I was going to do this sonogram on her — she's pregnant, right? — and she just starts crying on me. *Híjole*, Felice! This poor lady's got black-and-blue marks all over. I'm not kidding.

From her husband. Who else? Another one of those brides from across the border. And her family's all in Mexico.

Shit. You think they're going to help her? Give me a break. This lady doesn't even speak English. She hasn't been allowed to call home or write or nothing. That's why I'm calling you.

She needs a ride.

Not to Mexico, you goof. Just to the Greyhound. In San Anto.

No, just a ride. She's got her own money. All you'd have to do is drop her off in San Antonio on your way home. Come on, Felice. Please? If we don't help her, who will? I'd drive her myself, but she needs to be on that bus before her husband gets home from work. What do you say?

I don't know. Wait.

Right away, tomorrow even.

Well, if tomorrow's no good for you . . .

It's a date, Felice. Thursday. At the Cash N Carry off I-10. Noon. She'll be ready.

Oh, and her name's Cleófilas.

I don't know. One of those Mexican saints, I guess. A martyr or something. Cleófilas. C-L-E-O-F-I-L-A-S. Cle. O. Fi. Las. Write it down.

Thanks, Felice. When her kid's born she'll have to name her after us, right?

Yeah, you got it. A regular soap opera sometimes. *Qué vida, comadre. Bueno* bye.

All morning that flutter of half-fear, half-doubt. At any moment Juan Pedro might appear in the doorway. On the street. At the Cash N Carry. Like in the dreams she dreamed.

There was that to think about, yes, until the woman in the pickup drove up. Then there wasn't time to think about anything but the pickup pointed toward San Antonio. Put your bags in the back and get in.

But when they drove across the *arroyo*, the driver opened her mouth and let out a yell as loud as any mariachi. Which startled not only Cleófilas, but Juan Pedrito as well.

Pues, look how cute. I scared you two, right? Sorry. Should've warned you. Every time I cross that bridge I do that. Because of the name, you know. Woman Hollering. *Pues,* I holler. She said this in a Spanish pocked with English and laughed. Did you ever notice, Felice continued, how nothing around here is named after a woman? Really. Unless she's the Virgin. I guess you're only famous if you're a virgin. She was laughing again.

That's why I like the name of that *arroyo*. Makes you want to holler like Tarzan, right?

Everything about this woman, this Felice, amazed Cleófilas. The fact that she drove a pickup. A pickup, mind you, but when Cleófilas asked if it was her husband's, she said she didn't have a husband. The pickup was hers. She herself had chosen it. She herself was paying for it.

I used to have a Pontiac Sunbird. But most cars are for *viejas*. Pussy cars. Now this here is a *real* car.

What kind of talk was that coming from a woman? Cleófilas thought. But then again, Felice was like no woman she'd ever met. Can you imagine, when we crossed the *arroyo* she just started yelling like a crazy, she would say later to her father and brothers. Just like that. Who would've thought?

Who would've? Pain or rage, perhaps, but not a hoot like the one Felice had just let go. Makes you want to holler like Tarzan, Felice had said.

Then Felice began laughing again, but it wasn't Felice laughing. It was gurgling out of her own throat, a long ribbon of laughter, like water.

QUESTIONS FOR CRITICAL THINKING AND WRITING

1. In this story, Cleófilas, Chela, Dolores, Soledad, Graciela, and Felice are Cisneros's female characters. Felice, Cisneros writes, is unlike any woman Cleófilas has ever met. Explain what makes her different from the other women.

2. At one point, Cisneros describes Cleófilas's husband as "this man, this father, this rival, this keeper, this lord, this master, this husband till kingdom come." How do you understand the relationship of the husband and wife given this line and Cisneros's other descriptions?

3. **CONNECT TO ANOTHER READING.** Both Sandra Cisneros and Gloria Anzaldúa pepper their English writing with Spanish words and phrases. Do you feel the combination of these languages has the same effect in both the Cisneros story and Anzaldúa poem/essay? Why or why not?

4. *La Gritona* ("Woman Hollering") is the name of the creek behind Cleófilas's house in America. Cleófilas spends a good deal of time wondering about the woman it was named for and thinks perhaps she was hollering out of anger or pain. Write a short personal essay about a place name that is meaningful to you. The place can be a house, a street, a river, a part of the country, and so on. Consider why it received its name and why it has particular resonance for you.

STEPHEN CRANE

Stephen Crane (1871–1900) was an American novelist, short story writer, poet, and journalist born in New Jersey. He is perhaps best known for his Civil War novel *The Red Badge of Courage*, written without firsthand knowledge of the battlefield. Crane once said that his "chiefest desire was to write plainly and unmistakably, so that all men (and some women) might read and understand." Some of his best-known stories are "The Open Boat," "The Blue Hotel," "The Monster," and "The Bride Comes to Yellow Sky," and many writers, including Ernest Hemingway, were influenced by his work. Crane died from tuberculosis at age twenty-eight.

BEFORE YOU READ

In the following story Crane presents a classic western tale complete with trains, a saloon, a town marshal, and a gunslinger. What do you expect will happen in a story like this one about the Wild West? As you read, consider how "Yellow Sky" matches your expectations and also where it diverges from them.

The Bride Comes to Yellow Sky   *1898*

I

The great Pullman was whirling onward with such dignity of motion that a glance from the window seemed simply to prove that the plains of Texas were pouring eastward. Vast flats of green grass, dull-hued spaces of mesquit and cactus, little groups of frame houses, woods of light and tender trees, all were sweeping into the east, sweeping over the horizon, a precipice.

A newly married pair had boarded this coach at San Antonio. The man's face was reddened from many days in the wind and sun, and a direct result of his new black clothes was that his brick-colored hands were constantly performing in a most conscious fashion. From time to time he looked down respectfully at his attire. He sat with a hand on each knee, like a man waiting in a barber's shop. The glances he devoted to other passengers were furtive and shy.

The bride was not pretty, nor was she very young. She wore a dress of blue cashmere, with small reservations of velvet here and there, and with steel buttons abounding. She continually twisted her head to regard her puff sleeves, very stiff, straight, and high. They embarrassed her. It was quite apparent that she had cooked, and that she expected to cook, dutifully. The blushes caused by the careless scrutiny of some passengers as she had entered the car were strange to see upon this plain, under-class countenance, which was drawn in placid, almost emotionless lines.

They were evidently very happy. "Ever been in a parlor-car before?" he asked, smiling with delight.

"No," she answered; "I never was. It's fine, ain't it?"

"Great! And then after a while we'll go forward to the diner, and get a big lay-out. Finest meal in the world. Charge a dollar."

"Oh, do they?" cried the bride. "Charge a dollar? Why, that's too much — for us — ain't it, Jack?"

"Not this trip, anyhow," he answered bravely. "We're going to go the whole thing."

Later he explained to her about the trains. "You see, it's a thousand miles from one end of Texas to the other; and this train runs right across it, and never stops but four times." He had the pride of an owner. He pointed out to her the dazzling fittings of the coach; and in truth her eyes opened wider as she contemplated the sea-green figured velvet, the shining brass, silver, and glass, the wood that gleamed as darkly brilliant as the surface of a pool of oil. At one end a bronze figure sturdily held a support for a separated chamber, and at convenient places on the ceiling were frescoes in olive and silver.

To the minds of the pair, their surroundings reflected the glory of their marriage that morning in San Antonio; this was the environment of their new estate; and the man's face in particular beamed with an elation that made him appear ridiculous to the negro porter. This individual at times surveyed them from afar with an amused and superior grin. On other occasions he bullied them with skill in ways that did not make it exactly plain to them that they were being bullied. He subtly used all the manners of the most unconquerable kind of snobbery. He oppressed them; but of this oppression they had small knowledge, and they speedily forgot that infrequently a number of travelers covered them with stares of derisive enjoyment. Historically there was supposed to be something infinitely humorous in their situation.

"We are due in Yellow Sky at 3:42," he said, looking tenderly into her eyes.

"Oh, are we?" she said, as if she had not been aware of it. To evince surprise at her husband's statement was part of her wifely amiability. She took from a pocket a little silver watch; and as she held it before her, and stared at it with a frown of attention, the new husband's face shone.

"I bought it in San Anton' from a friend of mine," he told her gleefully.

"It's seventeen minutes past twelve," she said, looking up at him with a kind of shy and clumsy coquetry. A passenger, noting this play, grew excessively sardonic, and winked at himself in one of the numerous mirrors.

At last they went to the dining-car. Two rows of negro waiters, in glowing white suits, surveyed their entrance with the interest, and also the equanimity, of men who had been forewarned. The pair fell to the lot of a waiter who happened to feel pleasure in steering them through their meal. He viewed them with the manner of a fatherly pilot, his countenance radiant with benevolence. The patronage, entwined with the ordinary deference, was not plain to them. And yet, as they returned to their coach, they showed in their faces a sense of escape.

To the left, miles down a long purple slope, was a little ribbon of mist where moved the keening Rio Grande. The train was approaching it at an angle, and the apex was Yellow Sky. Presently it was apparent that, as the distance from Yellow Sky grew shorter, the husband became commensurately restless. His brick-red hands were more insistent in their prominence. Occasionally he was even rather absent-minded and far-away when the bride leaned forward and addressed him.

As a matter of truth, Jack Potter was beginning to find the shadow of a deed weigh upon him like a leaden slab. He, the town marshal of Yellow Sky, a man known, liked, and feared in his corner, a prominent person, had gone to San Antonio to meet a girl he believed he loved, and there, after the usual prayers, had actually induced her to marry him, without consulting Yellow Sky for any part of the transaction. He was now bringing his bride before an innocent and unsuspecting community.

Of course people in Yellow Sky married as it pleased them in accordance with a general custom; but such was Potter's thought of his duty to his friends, or of their idea of his duty, or of an unspoken form which does not control men in these matters, that he felt he was heinous. He had committed an extraordinary crime. Face to face with this girl in San Antonio, and spurred by his sharp impulse, he had gone headlong over all the social hedges. At San Antonio he was like a man hidden in the dark. A knife to sever any friendly duty, any form, was easy to his hand in that remote city. But the hour of Yellow Sky — the hour of daylight — was approaching.

He knew full well that his marriage was an important thing to his town. It could only be exceeded by the burning of the new hotel. His friends could not forgive him. Frequently he had reflected on the advisability of telling them by telegraph, but a new cowardice had been upon him. He feared to do it. And now the train was hurrying him toward a scene of amazement, glee, and reproach. He glanced out of the window at the line of haze swinging slowly in toward the train.

Yellow Sky had a kind of brass band, which played painfully, to the delight of the populace. He laughed without heart as he thought of it. If the citizens could dream of his prospective arrival with his bride, they would parade the band at the station and escort them, amid cheers and laughing congratulations, to his adobe home.

He resolved that he would use all the devices of speed and plainscraft in making the journey from the station to his house. Once within that safe citadel, he could issue some sort of vocal bulletin, and then not go among the citizens until they had time to wear off a little of their enthusiasm.

The bride looked anxiously at him. "What's worrying you, Jack?"

He laughed again. "I'm not worrying, girl; I'm only thinking of Yellow Sky."

She flushed in comprehension.

A sense of mutual guilt invaded their minds and developed a finer tenderness. They looked at each other with eyes softly aglow. But Potter often laughed the same nervous laugh; the flush upon the bride's face seemed quite permanent.

The traitor to the feelings of Yellow Sky narrowly watched the speeding landscape. "We're nearly there," he said.

Presently the porter came and announced the proximity of Potter's home. He held a brush in his hand, and, with all his airy superiority gone, he brushed Potter's new clothes as the latter slowly turned this way and that way. Potter fumbled out a coin and gave it to the porter, as he had seen others do. It was a heavy and muscle-bound business, as that of a man shoeing his first horse.

The porter took their bag, and as the train began to slow they moved forward to the hooded platform of the car. Presently the two engines and their long string of coaches rushed into the station of Yellow Sky.

"They have to take water here," said Potter, from a constricted throat and in mournful cadence, as one announcing death. Before the train stopped his eye had swept the length of the platform, and he was glad and astonished to see there was none upon it but the station-agent, who, with a slightly hurried and anxious air, was walking toward the water-tanks. When the train had halted, the porter alighted first, and placed in position a little temporary step.

"Come on, girl," said Potter, hoarsely. As he helped her down they each laughed on a false note. He took the bag from the negro, and bade his wife cling to his arm. As they slunk rapidly away, his hang-dog glance perceived that they were unloading the two trunks, and also that the station-agent, far ahead near the baggage-car, had turned and was running toward him, making gestures. He laughed, and groaned as he laughed, when he noted the first effect of his marital bliss upon Yellow Sky. He gripped his wife's arm firmly to his side, and they fled. Behind them the porter stood, chuckling fatuously.

II

The California express on the Southern Railway was due at Yellow Sky in twenty-one minutes. There were six men at the bar of the Weary Gentleman saloon. One was a drummer° who talked a great deal and rapidly; three were Texans who did not care to talk at that time; and two were Mexican sheep-herders, who did not talk as a general practice in the Weary Gentleman saloon. The barkeeper's dog lay on the board walk that crossed in front of the door. His head was on his paws, and he glanced drowsily here and there with the constant vigilance of a dog that is kicked on occasion. Across the sandy street were some vivid green grass-plots, so wonderful in appearance, amid the sands that burned near them in a blazing sun, that they caused a doubt in the mind. They exactly resembled the grass mats used to represent lawns on the stage. At the cooler end of the railway station, a man without a coat sat in a tilted chair and smoked his pipe. The fresh-cut bank of the Rio Grande circled near the town, and there could be seen beyond it a great plum-colored plain of mesquit.

Save for the busy drummer and his companions in the saloon, Yellow Sky was dozing. The new-comer leaned gracefully upon the bar, and recited many tales with the confidence of a bard who has come upon a new field.

drummer: Traveling salesman.

"—and at the moment that the old man fell downstairs with the bureau in his arms, the old woman was coming up with two scuttles of coal, and of course—"

The drummer's tale was interrupted by a young man who suddenly appeared in the open door. He cried: "Scratchy Wilson's drunk, and has turned loose with both hands." The two Mexicans at once set down their glasses and faded out of the rear entrance of the saloon.

The drummer, innocent and jocular, answered: "All right, old man. S'pose he has? Come in and have a drink, anyhow."

But the information had made such an obvious cleft in every skull in the room that the drummer was obliged to see its importance. All had become instantly solemn. "Say," said he, mystified, "what is this?" His three companions made the introductory gesture of eloquent speech; but the young man at the door forestalled them.

"It means, my friend," he answered, as he came into the saloon, "that for the next two hours this town won't be a health resort."

The barkeeper went to the door, and locked and barred it; reaching out of the window, he pulled in heavy wooden shutters, and barred them. Immediately a solemn, chapel-like gloom was upon the place. The drummer was looking from one to another.

"But, say," he cried, "what is this, anyhow? You don't mean there is going to be a gun-fight?"

"Don't know whether there'll be a fight or not," answered one man, grimly; "but there'll be some shootin'—some good shootin'."

The young man who had warned them waved his hand. "Oh, there'll be a fight fast enough, if any one wants it. Anybody can get a fight out there in the street. There's a fight just waiting."

The drummer seemed to be swayed between the interest of a foreigner and a perception of personal danger.

"What did you say his name was?" he asked.

"Scratchy Wilson," they answered in chorus.

"And will he kill anybody? What are you going to do? Does this happen often? Does he rampage around like this once a week or so? Can he break in that door?"

"No; he can't break down that door," replied the barkeeper. "He's tried it three times. But when he comes you'd better lay down on the floor, stranger. He's dead sure to shoot at it, and a bullet may come through."

Thereafter the drummer kept a strict eye upon the door. The time had not yet called for him to hug the floor, but, as a minor precaution, he sidled near the wall. "Will he kill anybody?" he said again.

The men laughed low and scornfully at the question.

"He's out to shoot, and he's out for trouble. Don't see any good in experimentin' with him."

"But what do you do in a case like this? What do you do?"

A man responded: "Why, he and Jack Potter—"

"But," in chorus the other men interrupted, "Jack Potter's in San Anton'."

"Well, who is he? What's he got to do with it?"

"Oh, he's the town marshal. He goes out and fights Scratchy when he gets on one of these tears."

"Wow!" said the drummer, mopping his brow. "Nice job he's got."

The voices had toned away to mere whisperings. The drummer wished to ask further questions, which were born of an increasing anxiety and bewilderment; but when he attempted them, the men merely looked at him in irritation and motioned him to remain silent. A tense waiting hush was upon them. In the deep shadows of the room their eyes shone as they listened for sounds from the street. One man made three gestures at the barkeeper; and the latter, moving like a ghost, handed him a glass and a bottle. The man poured a full glass of whisky, and set down the bottle noiselessly. He gulped the whisky in a swallow, and turned again toward the door in immovable silence. The drummer saw that the barkeeper, without a sound, had taken a Winchester from beneath the bar. Later he saw this individual beckoning to him, so he tiptoed across the room.

"You better come with me back of the bar."

"No thanks," said the drummer, perspiring; "I'd rather be where I can make a break for the back door."

Whereupon the man of bottles made a kindly but peremptory gesture. The drummer obeyed it, and, finding himself seated on a box with his head below the level of the bar, balm was laid upon his soul at sight of various zinc and copper fittings that bore a resemblance to armor-plate. The barkeeper took a seat comfortably upon an adjacent box.

"You see," he whispered, "this here Scratchy Wilson is a wonder with a gun — a perfect wonder; and when he goes on the war-trail, we hunt our holes — naturally. He's about the last one of the old gang that used to hang out along the river here. He's a terror when he's drunk. When he's sober he's all right — kind of simple — wouldn't hurt a fly — nicest fellow in town. But when he's drunk — whoo!"

There were periods of stillness. "I wish Jack Potter was back from San Anton'," said the barkeeper. "He shot Wilson up once — in the leg — and he would sail in and pull out the kinks in this thing."

Presently they heard from a distance the sound of a shot, followed by three wild yowls. It instantly removed a bond from the men in the darkened saloon. There was a shuffling of feet. They looked at each other. "Here he comes," they said.

III

A man in a maroon-colored flannel shirt, which had been purchased for purposes of decoration, and made principally by some Jewish women on the East Side of New York, rounded a corner and walked into the middle of the main street of Yellow Sky. In either hand the man held a long, heavy, blue-black revolver. Often he yelled, and these cries rang through a semblance of a deserted village, shrilly flying over the roofs in a volume that seemed to have no relation to the ordinary vocal strength of a man. It was as if the surrounding stillness formed the arch of a tomb over him. These cries of ferocious challenge rang against walls of silence. And his boots had red tops with gilded imprints, of the kind beloved in winter by little sledding boys on the hillsides of New England.

The man's face flamed in a rage begot of whisky. His eyes, rolling, and yet keen for ambush, hunted the still doorways and windows. He walked with the creeping movement of the midnight cat. As it occurred to him, he roared menacing information. The long revolvers in his hands were as easy as straws; they were removed with an electric swiftness. The little fingers of each hand played sometimes in a musician's way. Plain from the low collar of the shirt, the cords of his neck straightened and sank, straightened and sank, as passion moved him. The only sounds were his terrible invitations. The calm adobes preserved their demeanor at the passing of this small thing in the middle of the street.

There was no offer of fight—no offer of fight. The man called to the sky. There were no attractions. He bellowed and fumed and swayed his revolvers here and everywhere.

The dog of the barkeeper of the Weary Gentleman saloon had not appreciated the advance of events. He yet lay dozing in front of his master's door. At sight of the dog, the man paused and raised his revolver humorously. At sight of the man, the dog sprang up and walked diagonally away, with a sullen head, and growling. The man yelled, and the dog broke into a gallop. As it was about to enter the alley, there was a loud noise, a whistling, and something spat the ground directly before it. The dog screamed, and, wheeling in terror, galloped headlong in a new direction. Again there was a noise, a whistling, and sand was kicked viciously before it. Fear-stricken, the dog turned and flurried like an animal in a pen. The man stood laughing, his weapons at his hips.

Ultimately the man was attracted by the closed door of the Weary Gentleman saloon. He went to it and, hammering with a revolver, demanded drink.

The door remaining imperturbable, he picked a bit of paper from the walk, and nailed it to the framework with a knife. He then turned his back contemptuously upon this popular resort and, walking to the opposite side of the street and spinning there on his heel quickly and lithely, fired at the bit of paper. He missed it by a half inch. He swore at himself, and went away. Later he comfortably fusilladed the windows of his most intimate friend. The man was playing with this town; it was a toy for him.

But still there was no offer of fight. The name of Jack Potter, his ancient antagonist, entered his mind, and he concluded that it would be a glad thing if he should go to Potter's house, and by bombardment induce him to come out and fight. He moved in the direction of his desire, chanting Apache scalp-music.

When he arrived at it, Potter's house presented the same still front as had the other adobes. Taking up a strategic position, the man howled a challenge. But this house regarded him as might a great stone god. It gave no sign. After a decent wait, the man howled further challenges, mingling with them wonderful epithets.

Presently there came the spectacle of a man churning himself into deepest rage over the immobility of a house. He fumed at it as the winter wind attacks a prairie cabin in the North. To the distance there should have gone the sound of a tumult like the fighting of two hundred Mexicans. As necessity bade him, he paused for breath or to reload his revolvers.

IV

Potter and his bride walked sheepishly and with speed. Sometimes they laughed together shamefacedly and low.

"Next corner, dear," he said finally.

They put forth the efforts of a pair walking bowed against a strong wind. Potter was about to raise a finger to point the first appearance of the new home when, as they circled the corner, they came face to face with a man in a maroon-colored shirt, who was feverishly pushing cartridges into a large revolver. Upon the instant the man dropped his revolver to the ground and, like lightning, whipped another from its holster. The second weapon was aimed at the bridegroom's chest.

There was a silence. Potter's mouth seemed to be merely a grave for his tongue. He exhibited an instinct to at once loosen his arm from the woman's grip, and he dropped the bag to the sand. As for the bride, her face had gone as yellow as old cloth. She was a slave to hideous rites, gazing at the apparitional snake.

The two men faced each other at a distance of three paces. He of the revolver smiled with a new and quiet ferocity.

"Tried to sneak up on me," he said. "Tried to sneak up on me!" His eyes grew more baleful. As Potter made a slight movement, the man thrust his revolver venomously forward. "No, don't you do it, Jack Potter. Don't you move a finger toward a gun just yet. Don't you move an eyelash. The time has come for me to settle with you and I'm goin' to do it my own way, and loaf along with no interferin'. So if you don't want a gun bent on you, just mind what I tell you."

Potter looked at his enemy. "I ain't got a gun on me, Scratchy," he said. "Honest, I ain't." He was stiffening and steadying, but yet somewhere at the back of his mind a vision of the Pullman floated: the sea-green figured velvet, the shining brass, silver, and glass, the wood that gleamed as darkly brilliant as the surface of a pool of oil — all the glory of marriage, the environment of the new estate. "You know I fight when it comes to fighting, Scratchy Wilson; but I ain't got a gun on me. You'll have to do all the shootin' yourself."

His enemy's face went livid. He stepped forward, and lashed his weapon to and fro before Potter's chest. "Don't you tell me you ain't got no gun on you, you whelp. Don't tell me no lie like that. There ain't a man in Texas ever seen you without no gun. Don't take me for no kid." His eyes blazed with light, and his throat worked like a pump.

"I ain't takin' you for no kid," answered Potter. His heels had not moved an inch backward. "I'm takin' you for a damn fool. I tell you I ain't got a gun, and I ain't. If you're goin' to shoot me up, you better begin now; you'll never get a chance like this again."

So much enforced reasoning had told on Wilson's rage; he was calmer. "If you ain't got a gun, why ain't you got a gun?" he sneered. "Been to Sunday-school?"

"I ain't got a gun because I've just come from San Anton' with my wife. I'm married," said Potter. "And if I'd thought there was going to be any galoots like you prowling around when I brought my wife home, I'd had a gun, and don't you forget it."

"Married!" said Scratchy, not at all comprehending.

"Yes, married. I'm married," said Potter, distinctly.

"Married?" said Scratchy. Seemingly for the first time, he saw the drooping, drowning woman at the other man's side. "No!" he said. He was like a creature allowed a glimpse of another world. He moved a pace backward, and his arm, with the revolver, dropped to his side. "Is this the lady?" he asked.

"Yes; this is the lady," answered Potter.

There was another period of silence.

"Well," said Wilson at last, slowly, "I s'pose it's all off now."

"It's all off if you say so, Scratchy. You know I didn't make the trouble." Potter lifted his valise.

"Well, I 'low it's off, Jack," said Wilson. He was looking at the ground. "Married!" He was not a student of chivalry; it was merely that in the presence of this foreign condition he was a simple child of the earlier plains. He picked up his starboard revolver, and, placing both weapons in their holsters, he went away. His feet made funnel-shaped tracks in the heavy sand.

QUESTIONS FOR CRITICAL THINKING AND WRITING

1. Place names are important in Stephen Crane's "The Bride Comes to Yellow Sky," just as they are in Sandra Cisneros's "Woman Hollering Creek." Why do you think Crane calls his town "Yellow Sky"? Are there other place names of significance in this story? Explain.

2. How does Jack Potter imagine news of his marriage will affect the town of Yellow Sky? How does it affect Scratchy?

3. How is Potter perceived on the train? Is it important that the perception there is different from how he is viewed in Yellow Sky? Why or why not?

4. **CONNECT TO ANOTHER READING.** The Rio Grande is an important symbol to many Texan writers, and it appears in Crane's "The Bride Comes to Yellow Sky," McMurtry's "The Last Picture Show," and Anzaldúa's "The Homeland, Aztlán." In an essay, discuss the importance of the river in these writings. Include your own research on the history of the river and details about its importance to Texans over the years.

J. FRANK DOBIE

Folklorist James Frank Dobie (1888–1964) was born in Live Oak County, Texas. He graduated from Southwestern University in Georgetown, Texas, in 1910 and joined the faculty of the University of Texas at Austin in 1914 before leaving to fight in World War I. He held many liberal views that clashed with the politics of his state; in later years, while he worked as a columnist, Dobie made Texas a target in his writing. He wrote, "When I get ready to explain homemade fascism in America, I can take my example from the state capitol of Texas." His books and anthologies include *A Vaquero of the Brush Country*, *Coronado's Children*, *On the Open Range*, *The Flavor of Texas*, *The Longhorns*, *A Texan in England*, *The Voice of the Coyote*, *The Ben Lilly Legend*, *Up the Trail from Texas*, *I'll Tell You a Tale*, *Cow People*, and *Out of the Old Rock*, from which the following tale comes. President Lyndon Baines Johnson awarded Dobie the prestigious Medal of Freedom on September 14, 1964.

BEFORE YOU READ

In the following memoir, Dobie has recorded eighty-eight-year-old W. W. Burton's remembrance of his early range experiences—from the time when Texas first entered the Union as a state. Why might W. W. Burton's words be of interest to readers today? Do records of such lives and traditions preserve any important details of our nation's history?

W. W. Burton, An Old Trail Driver Tells His Story   1972

In 1852, my father bought a ranch out from the Brazos River above the present city of Waco, and I helped drive out six hundred head of cattle to the new range. I was only eight years old then; I don't know how long I had been riding. By the time I was twelve years old I considered myself a good rider and roper.

Sam Burton, my father, believed in letting his sons have a little sense knocked into them. A horse might be pitching with Otho, my kid brother. Mother would be screaming that he was being killed, and Pa would just read on as he sat there on the gallery, never looking up. He'd simply remark, "If Otho gets throwed, it won't do him no harm. He needs a little experience anyhow."

The settlers who did not build their houses at springs or on streams dug wells by hand. But in those days we had no windmills, and we drew water only for home use and for saddle horses and milch cows. Range stock watered at lakes and streams. Sometimes we made a little tank on a draw. We had no scrapers° to carry the dirt, so we used cowhides. A man or two spaded dirt onto a big dry hide; another man on horseback had his rope tied to the tail and when the hide was loaded he dragged it over to where the dam was to be made. It was easy to dump the dirt by pulling the hide back and over instead of straight forward. After the toughest ox hide had been dragged around in this manner for a while, it became as pliable as buckskin. Mother took two or three such soft hides from us boys and used them to place under mattresses. They were as warm as buffalo robes.

We had no horseshoes to speak of. If a horse went lame from being tenderfooted, we might turn him loose and catch another. But often we were where we couldn't let the horse go without risk of never finding him again. Then, the remedy was to take a hot iron and sear the tender part of the foot. It never seemed to hurt much. Many a time I've set a horse's foot down on a red-hot skillet lid, and he'd hold it there till I took him away. After that he'd mend up, and in two or three days I'd be riding him again.

Taking cattle through a rough country would make some of them tenderfooted, and on a drive to Missouri in 1859, we threw down some big steers and burned their feet and they got all right. . . .

About the only cattle we sold were grown steers. When a rancher gathered his steers to sell, he caught everything else in the same class running on his

---

scraper: An instrument drawn by oxen or horses for scraping up dirt for use in construction.

TEXAS LONG HORN STEER
HORNS MEASURING OVER 8 FEET TIP TO TIP
MORE THAN 9 FEET ALONG THE HORNS

DISPLAYED AT
FAMOUS BUCKHORN CURIO STORE
(*Originally The Buckhorn Saloon*)
SAN ANTONIO, TEXAS

OLD TEX

The Texas Longhorn. The original caption text for this circa 1939 postcard reads: "Old 'Tex,' the best known specimen of that hardy race of cattle, the famous TEXAS-LONGHORN, escaped the early day cowboys who herded and drove them to distant railroad shipping points. He roamed the prairies of Southwest Texas to an undetermined age and is now full body mounted as shown and stands as one of the outstanding exhibits in the Buckhorn Curio Store Museum, originally the Famous Buckhorn Bar in San Antonio, Texas."
© Lake County Museum/Corbis.

range and sold them too, keeping a book account of the various brands. Once a year there would be a meeting of stockmen to settle accounts. . . .

When beef buyers came to receive cattle, they brought along gold, sometimes in a money belt, sometimes in saddlebags, sometimes in a sack or a *morral*. While the cattle were being delivered, this money hung unprotected in camp or in some rancher's home. After the cattle were received, the gold pieces were counted out to the owner, maybe on a blanket, maybe right on the ground.

In 1859, I made my first drive up the trail. . . . The herd consisted of five hundred mature steers put up by seven neighboring ranchmen, one of whom was my father. . . .

Mot Donahue was the only grown man in the outfit, the other five of us being youngsters. We had four horses apiece, and the extra horses were driven right along with the cattle and herded with them. . . .

We crossed the Trinity River at Dallas, then just a wide place in the road. We crossed Red River at Rabbit Ford, as it was then called, though later it came to be known as Colbert's Ferry. An Indian had a little ferryboat, and crossed our wagon for a dollar. The boat was not big enough to hold both the oxen and the wagon, and so the oxen had to swim with the rest of us. We were now in the Indian Nation, but everything was quiet and we had no trouble. I do not remember having seen any other cattle than ours on the trail, but the route we traveled was well marked. It was called the Old Beef Trail. . . .

Our trail led on through Granny Gap, just a narrow pass in the Granny Mountains, and on to Springfield, a mere village then.

I don't remember what the cattle brought—probably around $50 a head. We boys had other fish to fry when we got to a town like Springfield, and left the selling to Mot Donahue. Each of us wore two six-shooters—I've got one of mine yet. We left Waco along in June and were back early in September. We drove slow going up, giving the steers plenty of time to fatten on the way. It took about two and a half months to make the trip up and about two weeks to come back. . . .

In 1861 the Burton family branded 1,100 calves. When the war was over and brother Otho and I got home we found only two hundred calves to brand. A great deal of the stock along the Brazos had been driven west by renegades, some of whom became cattle kings. But after the war cattle were worth next to nothing anyhow. Choice steers sold at $8 and $10 a head, and stock cattle could be purchased for a dollar or two.

It was about 1867 that our neighborhood had quite a bit of excitement over a slick rascal from the North, who came in, put up at the old Peter McLennan Hotel in Waco, and bought a string of cattle from surrounding ranchers. He had his outfit with him and was away and gone with the cattle before somebody discovered that the greenback money which had been paid out for the cattle—as well as the hotel bill—was all counterfeit. A posse was made up to follow him. I remember that I was in a cow camp at the time word of the cheating reached us. I and some other men left right away to join in the hunt.

Some of the posse caught the cattle at Red River. I don't know whether the counterfeit money man went up the river or down it, but I have always understood he did not go across it. There was a saying in those days that the law of Texas was at the end of a rope. . . .

Soon after the war ended, my brother Otho and I fixed up some picket pens at our old ranch north of Waco and began to road-brand herds from south Texas. We had complete equipment, including a long branding chute. It was a law, either written or unwritten, that after cattle crossed the Brazos they had to be road-branded. . . .

It was while we were branding out a herd of . . . big King Ranch steers that I first saw a Mexican whip a steer. One rough old steer absolutely refused to go out of the big pen into the chute pen. He would fight men on horseback and dodge into corners. A Mexican working for us named Celi said, "You say so, me fight that steer and make him go into chute."

"Go to it," I told him.

Celi grabbed up a fence rail and made for the steer on foot. The steer ran at him: the Mexican dodged, and as the animal went by let him have a lick on the backbone that tamed him considerably. In no time Celi was right up on that steer's side prodding him into the chute.

But before a man undertook to deal afoot with one of these long-horned, maddened critters, he had better know his business. Once a herd of them stampeded right in Waco. Only a few houses were there then, and brush grew in the streets. A baker stepped out of his shop and shooed at one of the steers. The steer made a lunge at him and caught him under the chin with a horn, the point coming out of the man's mouth. The steer was a heavy, strong devil, and he dragged the baker for two hundred yards before a cowboy shot him. The baker died. The steer was butchered and the meat given away.

QUESTIONS FOR CRITICAL THINKING AND WRITING

1. W. W. Burton's memoir is full of life details, some of which have resonance as Texas folklore. What sections of this passage are the most powerful? Why?

2. What does the anecdote about the "slick rascal from the North" indicate about regional differences at the time?

3. How were horses and cattle cared for by cattle drivers in early Texas?

4. **RESEARCH AND WRITE.** What does this memoir reveal about Burton and others like him who lived in Texas in the old days? Conduct some research into this era and cattle driving in Texas. In a brief essay, with Dobie's account in mind, analyze the life someone like Burton would have led on the range.

DAGOBERTO GILB

For biographical information on Dagoberto Gilb, see page 1 of the Introduction.

BEFORE YOU READ

In the following story (from *The Magic of Blood*) two characters become side-tracked from their workday. What factors influence the decisions that Alex and Carlos make? Why do they behave as they do? As you read, take note of Gilb's tone and use of dialogue. How does he portray his protagonists?

Truck   1994

In the center of the carpenter's shop was the table saw. As always, or almost, Martínez was holding a piece of wood against the fence, his straw cowboy hat a little low on his forehead, a cigarette slanted out the right side of his mouth, his eyes slit onto a bevel cut he was guiding through. A few of the men, carpenters and laborers, had hopped up and sat on the work table which L'ed two walls. Others stood near the radial-arm saw, a couple leaned against the drill press. Two more men hovered near Martínez, so full of admiration their expressions verged on love. Since Martínez had once been employed in a cabinet shop, he was the star of the show, the man called on for the fine jobs, when patience and delicacy were more important than speed and strength. These two men near him were especially impressed by his skill.

The table saw was loud, even louder when it was cutting, and nobody bothered much about talking with it engaged. But when the power was shut off and the motor wound down, the contrasting silence was dramatic. Modesty being another of Martínez's virtues, he liked to take the hushed moment at the center of the shop to remark on his just finished product with self-deprecation.

"It'll have to do," he pronounced, the cigarette between his lips waving up and down with each syllable. He held the cut piece there, eyeballing the length as he savored a drag off the unfiltered butt.

Blondie, the foreman, known jokingly as el mero güero, was at his wooden desk at another corner of the shop. In fact his blond hair was mostly gray. "Moya," he called, waving Alex over. Carlos Davis followed a step behind.

"You wanna buy it?" Blondie asked. He liked Alex. "It's almost new."

"It's a .357 Magnum?" Alex asked. Carlos was big-eyed over Alex's shoulder.

".44 Magnum. If you don't know the difference, you don't know."

"Can I see it?" Carlos asked.

Blondie's head went back and his eyebrows lifted, meaning no way. He didn't need to respond with words, and he seldom used them, a result, probably, of his not knowing any Spanish and working with so many men who knew so little English. He'd worked for the city over twenty years, and this was his last week. He handed the pistol to Alex. He liked Alex, liked his work, but he didn't trust Carlos. A few of the other men wandered over, including Martínez.

"I guess not," Alex told him as he babied it in his hands. "Sure wouldn't want it aimed at me."

Martínez—nobody used his first name—reached for the gun, and Alex passed it on. "Go right through two or three walls, I hear," he said. "Puts a hole in the man the size of a football, I hear."

Blondie nodded, indifferent to the information. "Good protection," he said. "I just wanna sell it."

"Not today," Alex apologized.

"I own a Remington shotgun," Martínez said. "It'll put a hole in the right places too."

"Yeah, well . . ." Blondie stared back at his desk, at a pile of work requisitions. "This one's for you," he told Alex. "A partition at the Armijo Center."

"Just me and Carlos?"

Blondie nodded. Then he shook some keys off the desk. "I'm going ahead and giving you this truck." It was the truck the shop had been promised a year earlier but had just got the week before. If Blondie hadn't retired, it would've been his to drive home. The new foreman didn't need one because he already had one.

Alex could feel Martínez's sigh of disapproval. He'd spend the rest of the day talking about what a mistake this was, how one of the other carpenters deserved it more.

"One thing," Blondie said, pulling the hand with the keys back to keep Alex's attention. He glanced over at Martínez, who was listening closer than he pretended, before he spoke. "Well, you know, or you should by now."

After he and Carlos slid plywood and 2x4s onto the bed of the truck, Alex picked up a skilsaw and a cord and some nails, then loaded them and his toolbox. It was a long drive from the city's yard in the rural Lower Valley to the Segundo Barrio. Alex, who was always in a hurry, was about to get on I-10. "N'hombre!" Carlos told him. "Go the long ways, make it happen slow." He'd dragged out the last word like he was talking about sex. Alex grinned and nodded and cruised North Loop, whiffing the damp smell of horses.

Carlos was excited about being in the truck—maybe the newest auto he'd ever been in, besides a police car, and it was close to two years old. "You see how I told you?" he said. "I told you about Blondie, how he'd listen. He knows how you're the best carpenter. He knows. He knows about that metiche Martínez too, how he talks pedo behind your back . . ."

"Forget about it, man," Alex said, cutting him short. "Let's forget about that dude."

Carlos had a habit of going too far, making fights. Not that he wasn't right about Martínez. And Blondie did honor Alex with one of the trucks—Urquidi drove the one-ton for the large jobs which most of the men went to, but now he and Martínez would be treated as equals for the smaller, two-man jobs. Still, Carlos exaggerated, just like he did about what a great carpenter Alex was. His exaggerations confused Alex as much as his confessions, like the one about stealing from the shop. A block plane, a Phillips screwdriver, some needle-nose pliers. Things did get lost, and probably other men had taken a tool or two. Carlos wasn't exactly wrong about this. But if Alex was sure it wasn't exactly right either, he didn't say so. He couldn't resist the admiration, seeming smart, or skilled, or whatever it was Carlos saw in him, and he didn't want to be a disappointment. And then, even though he was eight years older than Carlos, who was twenty, Alex carried a private respect for him. Alex might stand up and say he could hold his own, but Carlos had been raised real tough and done real bad, and that, like having been to war, was a strength that was always veiled and mysterious, envied by those who grew up on the easier side of the highway. All Alex had done to be this great carpenter was work for his cousin's construction company. He wanted this city job because it was steady—he was married and the father of two daughters, one not even a year old. It was Carlos's first job ever.

Carlos had grown up on Seventh Street. He came up behind one of the turquoise-framed screen doors, with only one light bulb, in that gray brick building, its seventy-year-old lintels and threshold tilted and sagging, the building across the street from the one painted sapphire, next to the ruby one, a block away from the one whose each apartment was a swath of brilliant Mexican color—the whole street woven with shades as bold and ornate and warm as an Indian blanket. Across the street from the Armijo Center, at the Boy's Club, Carlos stabbed a dude when he was eleven. Across from there, under the mural of Che Guevara, where all those gang placazos are sprayed in black, he soaked red bandannas, shut his eyes, and sniffed until his mind floated away like in a light wind.

"That's some stupid shit," Alex told him. "Make your brains turn to hamburger."

"Already I know now," Carlos said, serious, "but I didn't then." His lips bent sarcastically. "If they turned into tacos, that'd be something else, eh?"

Alex had been driving real slow down the street listening to Carlos, even went past the Armijo by a couple of blocks before he U-turned around.

"Park in the front, güey," Carlos said. "You got the city sign on the side. I wanna show off for my bros."

"It's a loading zone." Alex parked in the lot beside the building. He didn't want to mess up. That's what Blondie had meant: Martínez was behind the scenes saying how Alex was no better a carpenter than Carlos was his helper. "My grandma could do as well, and she's got cataracts," was how he'd say it. That the two got along was evidence of even fewer skills, since Martínez especially didn't like Carlos. The truck was Blondie's way of backing Alex.

Carlos shook his head displeased, pissed-off that he didn't get his way. "It'd be *bad* parking out in the front like we own the place."

"We ain't rock stars driving a limosine," Alex said, at moments like these wondering why he ever tried to work with the guy.

While Alex went through the glass front doors, Carlos hung back, doing a slow, unhappy strut outside in his chinos and white T-shirt. But once he did push the doors too and saw nobody else was around, he quickened his pace and dropped the attitude. They unloaded the material and tools and even flirted with the secretary while they worked — she was married, but she was all right. They built a partition to close off a small, lockable room for basketballs and pool sticks, ping-pong paddles, and the like. They didn't hang the door because it wouldn't be available until next week, but framed and plumbed and anchored and sheeted the wall with plywood, even fixed a couple of other things the secretary pointed out. All of it was done in three hours. Alex *was* fast, especially compared to the other city carpenters. It was all they were expected to do that day.

"Fucking Martínez," Carlos said out on the hardwood basketball courts. "That old dude would still be chopping the tree or some shit. His camaradas would be right at his culo. Oh, Mr. Mart-*tí*-nez, you do it so *good*. Maybe he'd still be hitting on a nail. Tac. Tac. Tac. Fucking put a dude to sleep, like to dead."

Alex had borrowed one of the basketballs. He'd played on his high-school basketball team, once in a while on the asphalt courts on the grounds of Austin High School with some old friends — he was shooting better now than he did back then, and he'd been good in high school.

"Andale, güey!" Carlos was shaking his head under the hoop. "What don't you do good?"

Alex was feeling fine because of his play, and of course the compliment helped. So fine it made him think of those things he didn't do anymore, that he'd left behind. He'd been doing right and that wasn't wrong. But he'd missed out too. He didn't get to shoot hoops often enough, and he'd forgotten how much fun it was messing around for no reason when — maybe even *because* — he knew he should be doing something better. He got all his girlfriends because he made baskets. His wife, who was the best-looking, sweetest girl he met in high school, first smiled at him because the ball swung in the net.

"Let's go to lunch," he said.

"Let's get some beer," Carlos suggested.

"Let's go to lunch and get beer too," Alex said.

They went down the street to the Jalisco Cafe and ordered the special and two beers each. It was still real early, and Alex didn't think it was a good idea to go back to the Armijo with nothing to do.

"Maybe we should just go back to the shop," Alex said.

"N'hombre! We ain't got nothing *there*. Better we do nothing *here*. How am I not right?"

It was one of these subjects that Alex didn't feel like arguing about. And Carlos was right — if they went back, they'd have to sit around bored, look for Blondie who probably wouldn't be around, even chance having to explain themselves if someone bigger came by.

Carlos told Alex about a shade tree they could park under, but first he made him stop at Mena's Bakery. Alex assumed it was for some cigarettes. Instead, Carlos came out with two quarts of beer.

"Are you crazy?" Alex said.

"Yessir, I am the crazy dude, at your service." Carlos unscrewed the cap from one and passed it to Alex. He was already having fun.

"We can't do this," Alex said.

Carlos put on his cholo slouch, his head drooping sideways and back. "It's not chiva, not even mota. It's not nothing, güey, just some *beer*."

Alex shook off his worry. He even felt ashamed for being afraid to do something as harmless as this. What kind of man was he becoming? It was no big deal. Who couldn't handle a little beer? And once he settled down and relaxed, he even liked it.

They kicked back under the shade tree for over an hour, then agreed to drive a long route back.

"Over there," Carlos said. Alex stopped the truck by a small grocery on Alameda. Carlos took a five from Alex for the peanuts that would disguise their breath.

He came back with a cocky smile and two more quarts of beer.

"No way, man," said Alex. "We're just going back. We can't walk in there after we drank these."

"I got the peanuts. And these were on sale." Carlos opened his. "Those dudes won't see nothing different in this dude."

Alex fought off his first impulses, even criticized himself again. Then Alex went ahead and opened the beer and drank and started enjoying himself—not quite like Carlos, who was chugging the bottle in a hurry. But Alex slipped into such a calm about it he drove with his mind on all kinds of things he'd wanted to do that he'd forgotten about, and he drove not thinking of much else other than this until he realized he'd driven too far, way east of the city complex. He both laughed and got mad at this lapse, looked both in front and in the rearview mirror. No cars were coming, and he turned left into the empty field on the other side of the street to turn around.

"What a stupid move, güey," Carlos said, irritated. He was more drunk than Alex. He was a sure bust—everybody would see him and know. "That pinche Martínez is gonna be out here to get us and be laughing in our face. What the fuck you do this for?"

They'd tried everything to get it out, but half the tire had dug itself into the sand. They'd tried putting rocks under it, chunks of wood. The tire spun, spraying sandy dirt.

"We ain't gonna get this truck no more," Carlos complained. "You lost us this truck."

Alex didn't disagree, or argue, or offer a word in defense. Like Martínez, Carlos was far away. Alex felt his feet leaving the ground, his arms cocking, the ball rolling off his fingers. As it spun away, arced, the touch of the ball stayed with him, and he felt the pleasure of it stretching the net, and clinging—a long time or short, depending on how he'd remember this, just like a first kiss.

QUESTIONS FOR CRITICAL THINKING AND WRITING

1. How are Alex and Carlos like or unlike each other? How are they like or unlike the older Martínez?

2. The truck was promised to the shop, which means it is for use by Martínez, Blondie, Alex, and Carlos. What is the importance of the truck to each of these men?

3. In this story, Gilb considers the lives of working-class Mexican American men. What does the story teach you about these men? What internal and external conflicts do they face?

4. **CONNECT TO ANOTHER READING.** Compare Gilb's use of humor in this story with that of another reading in this collection such as Macarena Hernández's essay "One Family, Two Homelands" (p. 90) or Molly Ivins's "Texas on Everything" (p. 17). How does the use of humor in these pieces contribute to (or detract from) the authors' purposes?

CHRISTINE GRANADOS

Christine Granados was born in El Paso, Texas, and is a freelance journalist and a stay-at-home mother of two. "The Bride" comes from her collection *Brides and Sinners in El Chuco*, which was published by University of Arizona Press in 2006. That year, she won the Alfredo Cisneros Del Moral Foundation Award, a grant given to new writers by Sandra Cisneros. *Brides and Sinners in El Chuco* was also a finalist in the short story category for the *ForeWord* Magazine Book of the Year, 2006, and received a notable book mention

© Ken Esten Cooke. Reprinted by permission.

in the Pima County Public Library Southwest Books of the Year awards in 2006. Granados earned her MFA in creative writing from Texas State University in San Marcos, Texas.

BEFORE YOU READ

In the following story, the narrator's sister Rochelle wants an "Anglo" wedding based on the idealized representations she finds in glossy magazines. As you read, do you expect Rochelle to have the wedding she desires?

The Bride   *2006*

When the month of June rolls around, I have to buy the five-pound bride magazine off the rack at the grocery store. The photographs of white dresses, articles with to-do lists, and advertisements for wedding planners remind me of my older sister Rochelle's wedding. She had been planning for her special day as far back as I can remember. Every year when she was a child, Rochelle dressed as a beautiful, blushing bride for Halloween. She sauntered her way down the hot, dusty streets of El Paso, accepting candy from our neighbors in her drawstring handbag. The white satin against Rochelle's olive skin made her look so pretty that I didn't mind the fact that we had to stop every three houses so she could empty the candy from her dainty bag into the ripped brown paper sack that I used for the journey. She had to drag me along with her—a reluctant Casper—because Mom made her, and because I could hold all her candy. Her thick black hair was braided, and she wore the trenzas in an Eva Perón-style moño. She spent hours in the bathroom, with her friend Prissy fixing her hair just right, only to cover her head with a white tulle veil.

As Rochelle did this, Mom would prepare my costume. Spent and uninspired after a long day at work, Mom would drape a sheet over me and cut out holes for eyes. It happened every year without fail. The fact that I couldn't make up my mind what I wanted to be for Halloween exasperated my already exhausted mother even more. In a matter of minutes, I would list the Bionic Woman, a wrestler, a linebacker, a fat man, all as potential getups before it was time to trick-or-treat.

Ro, on the other hand, had her bridal dress finished days in advance, and she'd wear it to school to show it off. When people opened their doors to us, they would say, "Ay, qué bonita la novia, and your little brother un fantasma tan scary." I'd have to clear things up at every house with "I'm not a boy." They would laugh and ask Rochelle if she had a husband. She would giggle and give them a name.

When she got too old for Halloween, she started getting serious about planning her own wedding. She bought bridal magazines and drew up plans, leaving absolutely no detail unattended. When it finally did happen, it was nothing like she had expected.

Rochelle was obsessed. Because all those ridiculous magazines never listed mariachis or dollar dances, she decided her wedding was going to have a string quartet, no bajo, horns, or anything, no dollar dance, and it was going to be in October. It was going to be a bland affair, outside in a tent, like the weddings up North in the "elegance of autumn" that she read about in the thick glossy pages of the magazines. I wasn't going to tell her there is no "elegance" to autumn in El Paso. Autumn is either "scramble a huevo on the hood of your car hot," or wind so strong the sand it blows stings your face and arms.

In the magazine pictures, all the people were white, skinny, and rich. All the women wore linen or silk slips that draped over their skeletal frames, and the men wore tuxedos or black suits and ties. She didn't take into account that in those pages, there was no tía Trini, who we called Teeny because, at five-foot-two, she weighed at least three hundred pounds. The slip dress Rochelle wanted everyone to wear would be swallowed in Teeny's cavernous flesh. And I never saw anyone resembling tío Lacho, who wore the burgundy tuxedo he got married in, two sizes too small, to every family wedding. The guests in the magazine weddings were polite and refined, with their long-stemmed wineglasses half full. No one ever got falling-down drunk and picked a fight, like Pilar. He would get so worked up someone would have to knock him out with a bottle of El Presidente. He was proud of the scars on his head, too, showing them off just before the big fight started.

Rochelle wanted tall white boys with jawbones that looked like they had been chiseled from stone to be her groomsmen; never mind the fact that we knew only one white boy, and he had acne so bad his face was blue. She also wanted her maid of honor to be pencil thin, although she would never admit it. Still, she was always dropping hints, telling her best friend, Prissy, that by the time they were twenty all their baby fat would be gone, and they would both look fabulous in their silk gowns. Never mind the fact that I, two years younger than Rochelle, could encircle my sister's bicep between my middle finger and thumb, and that Prissy rested her Tab colas on her huge stomach when she sat. My sister was in denial. And it wasn't just about her obese friend but about her entire life. She thought that if she planned every last detail of her wedding on paper, she could change who she was, who we were. Her lists drove me crazy.

She kept a running tally of the songs to be played by the band, adding and deleting as her musical tastes changed through the years. She carefully selected the food to be served to her guests. She resolutely decided what everyone in the family would be wearing. She even painstakingly chose what her dress would look like, down to the last sequin. But in order to marry, she needed a groom. And she was just as diligent about finding one as she was about the rest of the affair.

Every night before going to bed, she would pull out her pink wedding notebook and scratch a boy's name off her list of potential husbands. She went through two notebooks in one year. She was always on the lookout for husbands. One time, Rochelle and I spent an entire Saturday morning typing up fake raffle tickets to sell to Mike, who lived two blocks over. Ro had never met Mike, but she liked his broad shoulders—thought they'd look good in a tuxedo. So she made up a story that she was helping me sell raffle tickets for my softball team. Ro didn't let little things, like the truth, get in the way of her future. All the money raised would go into the team's travel budget. She even made up first-, second-, and third-place prizes. First place would be a color TV, second place, a dinner for two at Fortis Mexican Food Restaurant, and third, two tickets to the movies. She said Mike was going to win third place, and when she delivered his prize, she was going to suggest he take her to the movies since she was the one who sold him the winning ticket. I thought my sister was a genius, until we got to the door and knocked. When Mike answered, Ro delivered her lines like she had been selling raffle tickets all day long. When he told us he had no money, we were shocked. Ro didn't have a Plan B. Then, when his older brother came to the door and offered to buy all ten of the raffle tickets, we were speechless. All we could do was take his money, give him his stubs, and wish him luck. Ro was so upset her plan was a failure that she let me keep the ten dollars. Needless to say, Mike got scratched off her list.

Her blue notebook was where she compiled her guest list and either added or deleted a name depending on what had happened in school that day. I got scratched out six times in one month: for using all her sanitary napkins as elbow and knee pads while skating; for wearing her real silver concho belt and losing it at school; for telling Mom that Rochelle was giving herself hickeys on her arms; for peeking in her diary; for feeding her goldfish, Hughie, so much that he died; and especially, for telling her the truth about the food she planned to serve at her wedding. That final act kept me off the list for two months straight. She wanted finger foods like in Anglo weddings—sandwiches with the crusts cut off.

"Those cream cheese and cucumber sandwiches aren't going to cut it, Ro," I said through the cotton shirt I was taking off.

"My wedding is going to be classy," she yelled at me from across the room, where she was sitting on top of her bed, smoothing lotion on her arms. "If you don't want to eat my food, then you just won't be invited."

I laughed. Her nostrils were flaring pretty steady, and she was winding her middle finger around her ponytail. Then she reached under the mattress for her notebook, and my name, Lily, was off the list, just like that.

"I wouldn't want to go spend hours at some dumb wedding when I was half starving anyway. Everybody's going to faint before the dollar dance starts."

She stopped writing, "There isn't going to be a dollar dance." Then she wrinkled her wide nose, "Too gauche."

When I came back into the room after I had looked up the word, I told her, "I'm telling Mom you think she's tacky. You're carrying your gringa kick too far." Before shutting the bedroom door, I poked my head in and yelled, "I'm glad I'm not invited. I don't want to go to no white wedding."

Later, I asked her how she expected to go on her Hawaii honeymoon without a dollar dance. "You plan on selling the cucumber sandwiches at the wedding?"

She wiped the sarcastic smile off my face when she said, "No. I'm going to have a money tree." I told her that she was ridiculous and that she was going to be a laughingstock, not knowing how close my words were to the truth.

She didn't care what anyone thought. She said her wedding was hers, and it was one thing no one could ruin.

She kept up her lists as usual, but stopped physically adding to them in tenth grade — dropped and discarded as "too childish." By then, the lists were committed to memory, and I knew that she mentally scratched ex-friends and ex-boyfriends off of it. Lance, Rubén, Abraham, Artie, Oscar, Henry, Joel, and who knows who else had all been potential grooms.

It turned out to be Angel. He was beautiful, too — the Mexican version of the blond grooms in her magazines, right down to the cleft in his chin. He was perfect as long as he didn't smile, because when he smiled, his chipped, discolored front tooth showed. Rochelle worried about it all the time. She'd pull out photographs they had taken together, and the ones he had given her, to study them, trying to figure out the right camera angle that would hide his flaw. Anytime she mentioned getting it capped, he would roll his large almond-shaped eyes and smile. They would kiss and that would be the end of the discussion.

I knew this because Rochelle always had to drag me along on her dates. It was the only way our mother would allow her out of the house with a boy. I was a walking-and-talking birth control device. When we got home, I would replay the night's events for my mother. Funny, Ro relished the details of her wedding, but she never could stand for my instant replay of her dates. She would storm out of the living room when I would begin and slam the door to our bedroom. I usually had to sleep on the couch after our dates.

On prom night, Rochelle was allowed to go out with Angel alone, and she was so excited that she let me watch her dress for the big event. Tía Trini came over and rolled her hair, Prissy was there with her Tab in hand for moral support, and Mom was making last minute alterations to her gown. It was a salmon-colored version of her wedding dress. After she was teased, tweezed, and tucked, she looked like a stick of cotton candy from the top of her glittered hair down to her pink sling-back heels. When Angel saw her, he licked his lips like he was going to devour her.

Because I, her birth control device, wasn't in place during this date, the two got married when she was only a junior in high school, and she was four months pregnant. Rochelle and Angel drove thirty minutes to Las Cruces to be married by the justice of peace, with Mom in the back seat bawling. Even though Rochelle didn't get her elegant autumn wedding, she stood before Judge

Grijalva in her off-white linen pantsuit, which was damp on the shoulder and smeared with Mom's mascara, erect and with as much dignity as if she were under a tent at the Chamizal. It didn't matter to her that the groom wore his blue Dickie work pants with matching shirt that had his name stitched in yellow onto the pocket. She looked at him like they were the only two people inside the closet-sized courtroom.

She didn't even blink when a baby began to wail in her ear during "Do you take this man . . ."

And she never took her eyes off Angel when the woman next in line to get married, who was dressed in a skin-tight, leopard-print outfit, said, "Let's get this show on the road already. Kiss her, kiss her already."

And it didn't bother Rochelle that after Angel kissed her, he looked at his watch and said, "Vámonos. I need to get back to work," because he needed to get back to Sears before the evening rush.

QUESTIONS FOR CRITICAL THINKING AND WRITING

1. What is Lily's opinion of Rochelle's wedding aspirations? Why is she uniquely able to judge her circumstances? How would the story differ if Rochelle was the narrator?

2. How does Rochelle picture her wedding when she is a girl? Do any of those ideas and dreams carry over into her actual wedding?

3. **CONNECT TO ANOTHER READING.** Both Sandra Cisneros's "Woman Hollering Creek" and Christine Granados's "The Bride" follow the stories of young women whose ideas about weddings and marriage are based on media representations. In a short essay, compare the two young brides in these short stories. Consider why the *telenovelas* they watch and magazines they read are so influential. Do the characters' beliefs about weddings/marriage change over the course of the stories? How so?

JOHN GRAVES

John Graves was born in Fort Worth, Texas, in 1920 and holds degrees from Rice and Columbia universities. Inspired by a trip down the Brazos River, *Goodbye to a River: A Narrative*, the source of the following excerpt, won the Carr P. Collins Award of the Texas Institute of Letters and was nominated for a National Book Award. Graves's nonfiction often concerns his home state of Texas and is known for its blend of history, fiction, and observation. In addition to publishing books, he has published widely in magazines and anthologies over the years. Graves currently lives in the hill country of Texas, which he describes in his book *Hard Scrabble: Observations on a Patch of Land*.

BEFORE YOU READ

In the following passage from *Goodbye to a River*, Graves discusses what it means to account for one's roots. How much does where we're from have to do with who we are?

From *Goodbye to a River*   1961

Origin being as it is an accident outside the scope of one's will, I tend not to seek much credit for being a Texan. Often (breathes there a man?) I can work up some proud warmth about the fact that I indubitably am one. A lot of the time, though, I'd as soon be forty other kinds of men I've known. I've lived much away from that region, and have liked most of the places I've lived in. I used to know who the good bullfighters were and why they were good. I'm familiar with the washed silent streets of Manhattan at five o'clock in the morning, and what Los Angeles promises in the evening when you're young with money on your hip, and once almost saw the rats change sewers swarmingly in Paris, and did see dawn wash the top of the old wall at Avila. . . . I've waked in the green freshness of mountain mornings in tropical lands, and have heard the strange birds cry, and the street venders, and maybe music somewhere, and have felt the hit of it like a fist in my stomach, going sleepy-eyed out onto a balcony under the green mountains and above flame-flower trees to thank God for life and for being there. And I'm glad I have.

If a man couldn't escape what he came from, we would most of us still be peasants in Old World hovels. But if, having escaped or not, he wants in some way to know himself, define himself, and tries to do it without taking into account the thing he came from, he is writing without any ink in his pen. The provincial who cultivates only his roots is in peril, potato-like, of becoming more root than plant. The man who cuts his roots away and denies that they were ever connected with him withers into half a man. . . . It's not necessary to like being a Texan, or a Midwesterner, or a Jew, or an Andalusian, or a Negro, or a hybrid child of the international rich. It is, I think, necessary to know in that crystal chamber of the mind where one speaks straight to oneself that one is or was that thing, and for any understanding of the human condition it's probably necessary to know a little about what the thing consists of.

Questions for Critical Thinking and Writing

1. Why does Graves catalog the various places where he's lived in the first paragraph of the passage? What effect does that have on the argument he's making?

2. Why, according to Graves, is it important to know where you came from? Why might someone want to "escape what he came from"?

3. **CONNECT TO ANOTHER READING.** Consider the passages from other autobiographical works in this anthology. Do those writers "know in that crystal chamber of the mind where one speaks straight to oneself that one is or was that thing," as Graves puts it, in *Goodbye to a River*? In a short essay, choose one essay/memoir you've read in this anthology, and explain how the writer is in line or not in line with Graves's point of view.

O. Henry

William Sydney Porter (O. Henry) (1862–1910) was born in North Carolina and moved to Texas in 1882. While beginning his career as a writer, O. Henry lived in Austin and worked odd jobs. He once worked as a draftsman at the First National Bank of Austin and was accused of embezzlement but was not indicted. After the author moved to Houston, First National Bank of Austin was audited, and he was arrested. He continued to publish stories while in prison and was released in 1901; he died nine years later of causes related to alcoholism. During his lifetime, O. Henry was internationally known for his writing. Some of his most famous stories are "The Gift of the Magi," "The Ransom of Red Chief," "A Municipal Report," "The Cop and the Anthem," "After Twenty Years," and "Compliments of the Season." The following short story, "Jimmy Hayes and Muriel," appeared in O. Henry's collection *Sixes and Sevens*, first published in 1903.

Before You Read

What impression of the Texas Rangers do you get from this story? What is the purpose of this tale? How does O. Henry's version of the Texas Rangers jive with those you are aware of? With those of other writers in this anthology?

Jimmy Hayes and Muriel   1903

Supper was over, and there had fallen upon the camp the silence that accompanies the rolling of corn-husk cigarettes. The water hole shone from the dark earth like a patch of fallen sky. Coyotes yelped. Dull thumps indicated the rocking-horse movements of the hobbled ponies as they moved to fresh grass. A half-troop of the Frontier Battalion of Texas Rangers were distributed about the fire.

A well-known sound — the fluttering and scraping of chaparral against wooden stirrups — came from the thick brush above the camp. The rangers listened cautiously. They heard a loud and cheerful voice call out reassuringly:

"Brace up. Muriel, old girl, we're 'most there now! Been a long ride for ye, ain't it, ye old antediluvian handful of animated carpet-tacks? Hey, now, quit a tryin' to kiss me! Don't hold on to my neck so tight — this here paint hoss ain't any too shore-footed, let me tell ye. He's liable to dump us both off if we don't watch out."

Two minutes of waiting brought a tired "paint" pony single-footing into camp. A gangling youth of twenty lolled in the saddle. Of the "Muriel" whom he had been addressing, nothing was to be seen.

"Hi, fellows!" shouted the rider cheerfully. "This here's a letter fer Lieutenant Manning."

He dismounted, unsaddled, dropped the coils of his stake-rope, and got his hobbles from his saddle-horn. While Lieutenant Manning, in command, was reading the letter, the new-comer rubbed solicitously at some dried mud in the loops of the hobbles, showing a consideration for the forelegs of his mount.

"Boys," said the lieutenant, waving his hand to the rangers, "this is Mr. James Hayes. He's a new member of the company. Captain McLean sends him down from El Paso. The boys will see that you have some supper, Hayes, as soon as you get your pony hobbled."

The recruit was received cordially by the rangers. Still, they observed him shrewdly and with suspended judgment. Picking a comrade on the border is done with ten times the care and discretion with which a girl chooses a sweet-heart. On your "side-kicker's" nerve, loyalty, aim and coolness your own life may depend many times.

After a hearty supper, Hayes joined the smokers about the fire. His appearance did not settle all the questions in the minds of his brother rangers. They saw simply a loose, lank youth with tow-colored sunburned hair and a berry-brown, ingenuous face that wore a quizzical, good-natured smile.

"Fellows," said the new ranger, "I'm goin' to interduce to you a lady friend of mine. Ain't ever heard anybody call her a beauty, but you'll all admit she's got some fine points about her. Come along, Muriel!"

He held open the front of his blue flannel shirt. Out of it crawled a horned frog. A bright red ribbon was tied jauntily around her spiky neck. It crawled to its owner's knee and sat there motionless.

"This here Muriel," said Hayes, with an oratorical wave of his hand, "has got qualities. She never talks back, she always stays at home, and she's satisfied with one red dress for every day and Sunday, too."

"Look at that blame insect!" said one of the rangers with a grin. "I've seen plenty of them horny frogs, but I never knew anybody to have one for a side-partner. Does the blame thing know you from anybody else?"

"Take it over there and see," said Hayes.

The stumpy little lizard known as the horned frog is harmless. He has the hideousness of the prehistoric monsters whose reduced descendant he is, but he is gentler than the dove.

The ranger took Muriel from Hayes's knee and went back to his seat on a roll of blankets. The captive twisted and clawed and struggled vigorously in his hand. After holding it for a moment or two, the ranger set it upon the ground. Awkwardly, but swiftly, the frog worked its four oddly moving legs until it stopped close by Hayes's foot.

"Well, dang my hide!" said the other ranger. "The little cuss knows you. Never thought them insects had that much sense!"

Jimmy Hayes became a favorite in the ranger camp. He had an endless store of good nature, and a mild, perennial quality of humor that is well adapted to camp life. He was never without his horned frog. In the bosom of his shirt during rides, on his knee or shoulder in camp, under his blankets at night, the ugly little beast never left him.

Jimmy was a humorist of a type that prevails in the rural South and West. Unskilled in originating methods of amusing or in witty conceptions, he had hit upon a comical idea and clung to it reverently. It had seemed to Jimmy a very funny thing to have about his person, with which to amuse his friends, a tame horned frog with a red ribbon around its neck. As it was a happy idea, why not perpetuate it?

The sentiments existing between Jimmy and the frog cannot be exactly determined. The capability of the horned frog for lasting affection is a subject upon which we have had no symposiums. It is easier to guess Jimmy's feelings. Muriel was his chef d'oeuvre of wit, and as such he cherished her. He caught flies for her, and shielded her from sudden northers. Yet his care was half self-ish, and when the time came she repaid him a thousandfold. Other Muriels have thus overbalanced the light attentions of other Jimmies.

Not at once did Jimmy Hayes attain full brotherhood with his comrades. They loved him for his simplicity and drollness, but there hung above him a great sword of suspended judgment. To make merry in camp is not all of a ranger's life. There are horse-thieves to trail, desperate criminals to run down, braves to battle with, bandits to rout out of the chaparral, peace and order to be compelled at the muzzle of a six-shooter. Jimmy had been "most generally a cow-puncher," he said; he was inexperienced in ranger methods of warfare. Therefore the rangers speculated apart and solemnly as to how he would stand fire. For, let it be known, the honor and pride of each ranger company is the individual bravery of its members.

For two months the border was quiet. The rangers lolled, listless, in camp. And then—bringing joy to the rusting guardians of the frontier—Sebastiano Saldar, an eminent Mexican desperado and cattle-thief, crossed the Rio Grande with his gang and began to lay waste the Texas side. There were indications that Jimmy Hayes would soon have the opportunity to show his mettle. The rangers patrolled with alacrity, but Saldar's men were mounted like Lochinvar, and were hard to catch.

One evening, about sundown, the rangers halted for supper after a long ride. Their horses stood panting, with their saddles on. The men were frying bacon and boiling coffee. Suddenly, out of the brush, Sebastiano Saldar and his gang dashed upon them with blazing six shooters and high-voiced yells. It was a neat surprise. The rangers swore in annoyed tones, and got their Winchesters busy; but the attack was only a spectacular dash of the purest Mexican type. After the florid demonstration the raiders galloped away, yelling, down the river. The rangers mounted and pursued; but in less than two miles the fagged ponies labored so that Lieutenant Manning gave the word to abandon the chase and return to camp.

Then it was discovered that Jimmy Hayes was missing.

Someone remembered having seen him run for his pony when the attack began, but no one had set eyes on him since. Morning came, but no Jimmy. They searched the country around, on the theory that he had been killed or wounded, but without success. Then they followed after Saldar's gang, but it seemed to have disappeared. Manning concluded that the wily Mexican had recrossed the river after his theatric farewell. And, indeed, no further depredations from him were reported.

This gave the rangers time to nurse a soreness they had. As has been said, the pride and honor of the company is the individual bravery of its members. And now they believed that Jimmy Hayes had turned coward at the whiz of Mexican bullets. There was no other deduction. Buck Davis pointed out that not a shot was fired by Saldar's gang after Jimmy was seen running for his horse. There was no way for him to have been shot. No, he had fled from his first fight, and afterward he would not return, aware that the scorn of his comrades would be a worse thing to face than the muzzles of many rifles.

So Manning's detachment of McLean's company, Frontier Battalion, was gloomy. It was the first blot on its escutcheon. Never before in the history of the service had a ranger shown the white feather. All of them had liked Jimmy Hayes, and that made it worse.

Days, weeks, and months went by, and still that little cloud of unforgotten cowardice hung above the camp.

Nearly a year afterward—after many camping grounds and many hundreds of miles guarded and defended—Lieutenant Manning, with almost the same detachment of men, was sent to a point only a few miles below their old camp on the river to look after some smuggling there. One afternoon, while they were riding through a dense mesquite flat, they came upon a patch of open hog-wallow prairie. There they rode upon the scene of an unwritten tragedy.

In a big hog-wallow lay the skeletons of three Mexicans.

Their clothing alone served to identify them. The largest of the figures had once been Sebastiano Saldar. His great, costly sombrero, heavy with gold ornamentation — a hat famous all along the Rio Grande — lay there pierced by three bullets. Along the ridge of the hog-wallow rested the rusting Winchesters of the Mexicans — all pointing in the same direction.

The rangers rode in that direction for fifty yards. There, in a little depression of the ground, with his rifle still bearing upon the three, lay another skeleton. It had been a battle of extermination. There was nothing to identify the solitary defender. His clothing — such as the elements had left distinguishable — seemed to be of the kind that any ranchman or cowboy might have worn.

"Some cow-puncher," said Manning, "that they caught out alone. Good boy! He put up a dandy scrap before they got him. So that's why we didn't hear from Don Sebastiano any more!"

And then, from beneath the weather-beaten rags of the dead man, there wriggled out a horned frog with a faded red ribbon around its neck, and sat upon the shoulder of its long quiet master. Mutely it told the story of the untried youth and the swift "paint" pony — how they had outstripped all their comrades that day in the pursuit of the Mexican raiders, and how the boy had gone down upholding the honour of the company.

The ranger troop herded close, and a simultaneous wild yell arose from their lips. The outburst was at once a dirge, an apology, an epitaph, and a paean of triumph. A strange requiem, you may say, over the body of a fallen comrade; but if Jimmy Hayes could have heard it he would have understood.

QUESTIONS FOR CRITICAL THINKING AND WRITING

1. Why do you think O. Henry describes Jimmy's attentions to Muriel as "half selfish"?

2. O. Henry has written his characters' dialogue in dialect. What can you tell about the characters from the way they speak?

3. At the end of the story, what has happened between Jimmy Hayes and the three Mexicans found by the Rangers? What is the ending of this tale meant to convey?

4. **CONNECT TO ANOTHER READING.** The organization known as the Texas Rangers was originally formed to protect Stephen Austin's colony and other settlers living on the Texas frontier. Read the description of the Rangers in O. Henry's story alongside those of Américo Paredes (p. 133) and Walter Prescott Webb (p. 29). Create an outline that shows your understanding of the law enforcement organization — who they were, how they lived, who and how they fought, and so on. In your subsets, include quoted material from the texts. As an extension of this assignment, compare and contrast the portrayal of the Texas Rangers in the works mentioned above as well as with other sources, including popular culture (television, movies, advertising, etc.). How does the mythology compare to actual history?

Macarena Hernández

Macarena Hernández was born in Roma, Texas, grew up in La Joya, and now lives in Dallas. She has an undergraduate degree from Baylor University and a master's from the University of California, Berkeley. Hernández has written for the *Dallas Morning News*, the *San Antonio Express-News*, the *New York Times*, the *Philadelphia Inquirer*, and the *Los Angeles Times*. She received national attention in 2003 when a *New York Times* reporter plagiarized her work. Her memoir "One Family, Two Homelands" was published in the *San Antonio Express-News* in 2004.

BEFORE YOU READ

In the following essay, Hernández explores the stories and obsessions of her Mexican family living in Texas. How does being part of more than one culture affect someone growing up in the United States? How are we shaped by our families' pasts?

One Family, Two Homelands 2004

Big City Girl

My mother has her mother's small and delicate nose. And she has her father's sagging eyelids and his strong and stubborn ways. She is the one who tells Uelito José María *sus verdades*, the truths our family has always preferred to ignore. Still, after my grandmother dies, he comes to live with her.

"If you don't want me here I can go back to the rancho," Uelito José María says usually after my mother has reminded him that she is no longer a little girl, he can't tell her what to do. My grandfather is a *picabuche*, poking at my mother until she snaps.

"You should be grateful you had all those children in Mexico," she tells him in a voice armed with confidence, knowing my grandfather is another man, one who now admits his faults. "If you had had them in the United States, you would still be working to pay child support." My grandfather says my mother's *caracter fuerte*, strong character, comes from his mother, Uelita Lola. One look at a pregnant woman's belly and Uelita Lola, a midwife since she was 13, could tell whether she was carrying a boy or a girl. She was hardly ever wrong.

"My mother said your mother would be a man because of how she was sitting in the womb. She was upright," my grandfather tells me proudly. "Your mother wasn't a man but she worked like one. She's fierce, she's a workhorse. You can't pick on her because she defends herself."

Four months before my mother was born, Uelita Cecilia's world dissolved into darkness: *se oscurecio*. In the spring of 1940, a violent thunderstorm pummeled northern Nuevo Leon. My grandmother Cecilia and her sister-in-law, Juanita Alaniz, were caught in the winds of a tornado as the two walked home. They had spent the morning in La Lajilla, where they had gone to send a letter to my grandfather, who was in jail. It was a stupid thing, my grandfather says, to shoot at a passing car from the brush one afternoon as he and a friend hunted for quail to sell. They were arrested soon after and were kept locked up even though my grandfather and his friend denied it. Uelita Cecilia and her sister-in-law were halfway through the two-hour walk and still a ways from home when the storm caught them.

"It was horrible," recalls the now 85-year-old Juanita. "You could see the big cloud chasing after us. We were soaked and we lost our shoes as we ran, trying to get away. We had to stop at someone's house so they could help us pluck the (mesquite and cactus) thorns from our feet and legs."

My grandmother believed the shocking fright, susto, if not prayed away, would later revisit in the form of sickness. Soon after the storm, my grandmother began experiencing sharp *punsadas*, pulsations, behind her eyes. Within a few months, she was blind. My grandmother was still blind when my mother was born in the fall of 1941. No one remembers how long she remained blind, only that a healer from La Ceja helped cure her blindness. Still, for the rest of her life, my grandmother would blame that tornado for all her physical troubles.

Death and More Death

Mexicans are obsessed with death.

"If you don't bury me *en el rancho* I will come back after I die and pull your feet in the middle of the night," my mother told us. She would remind us to take her back to Mexico, especially around the first two days of November, when we celebrate Día de los Muertos. On the Day of the Dead, the cemetery in the rancho fills with people, most of whom haven't visited all year.

The first time I discussed death with my mother I was 5 and my pet chicken had just died. My mother was raising a dozen of them in our La Joya backyard, which was infested with fire ants. I found my black hen lying flat and stiff underneath my mother's washing machine outside our house, not long after she had sprinkled ant poison that resembled chicken feed. I cried for days. My mother reassured me that my nameless chicken was in heaven. But I kept crying.

"Por favor, Macarena!" she told me. "Please leave those tears for the day I die. When I die there will be no tears left for me."

Every year around Day of the Dead, my parents also visited my brother Ramiro's gravesite at La Piedad cemetery in McAllen. They would tie a small bouquet of plastic flowers to the green metal nameplate marking his grave. They never bought him a marble headstone because they didn't intend for him to stay there.

Ramiro, my mother's seventh child, arrived in early November 1971 while my father was working back in Mexico and my mother was at a relative's house in McAllen. My tío Baldo and tía Queta rushed her to a Mission clinic when her contractions came. When the clinic staff turned her away, her relatives drove her to Starr County, 35 miles west of Mission. They went in search of a midwife, who wasn't home. They drove back to Mission and found another midwife who sent my mother to the hospital after she began bleeding. My mother used Ramiro's first baby outfit—the yellow one she planned to take him home from the hospital in—to stop the blood from spilling onto the seats of the car. He drowned in her blood just before he was delivered. My mother was in the hospital when my father and his brother Rafael buried my brother at La Piedad cemetery, a narrow strip of graves now squeezed between the city airport and a row of warehouses.

"When I die," my mother would tell us, "I want you to take his *huecitos* (little bones) and bury them with me in Mexico. I don't want his gravesite to be forgotten."

In Mexico, my mother has always said, they respect the dead. *Aquí*, no. Here, they don't. For La Ceja, Altamira, Serafin and La Reforma, the cemetery is the meeting point, the one place where at least once a year, on Día de los Muertos, those who left come home to reunite with those still here. We forget our ranchos are dying. There, as a family, we reconnect with our dead. The marble gets polished and the photographs encased in glass are dusted. That is the only time the grass is trimmed and the weeds are yanked. The handful of people who still live here collect *donaciones*, paid mostly in dollars. One year, they paid for an outhouse.

When my mother was a teenager, the biggest dances of the year were held at the school during the Day of the Dead. Young couples danced as Los Hermanos Flores from Altamira played their *huapangos* and *rancheras*, while the mothers sold carne guisada plates. By the 1980s, those lively dances had faded into memory, as old and unfamiliar as the painted portraits of long-dead relatives that hung in my grandmother's house. No one gets married there anymore and there are hardly any children.

It was the drought that followed Hurricane Gilbert in 1988 that finally killed the ranchos, my grandfather says. The drought lasted more than a decade, forcing many to abandon their fields. It wiped out the agricultural industry, dominated by a few families that every year shipped out tons of watermelon, canteloupe, sorghum and corn to nearby Monterrey and as far south as Guadalajara and Mexico City. Some had no choice but to sell their cattle and land. In Comales, fishermen's wives made pilgrimages to the reservoir, where they begged God to open the skies. By then, only my grandfather and grandmother were left on our family rancho. The rancho's cemetery is the only gathering place left.

We know my father wanted to be buried there, close to his mother and grandmother, but unlike my mother, he didn't plan his funeral, only prayed for a quick death. "The day I die, these kids are going to do whatever they want," he would say. "I won't know the difference. I'll be dead."

One Tuesday night in August 1998, as he drove home from my brother's house where he had just dropped off a grandson's carseat, an 18-wheeler smashed into my father's car on the corner of Esperanza Street. He died instantly. My father and I were just starting to understand each other. Just three months earlier, he had watched me accept my master's degree from the University of California at Berkeley, just north of where my family once picked grapes.

My siblings were torn between burying him in Mexico or in the United States, where all of us live. In the end, we buried him in Mexico, a few feet from his parents' graves and his beloved grandmother Manuela, and next to his younger brother Enrique, who also died in a car accident nine years earlier. The Hernandezes, like their rancho, El Puente, have had short and sad lives, I tell my mother.

The small ranching community where my father's family first settled died decades before anyone in La Ceja could ever imagine their rancho suffering the same fate. All that is left of my father's childhood home, where his parents raised eight children, are the hollow walls of crumbling cinderblock. Not long after my father died, my mother abandoned her dream of a rancho life by the arroyo. These days, she just asks that we bury her next to him, by the main gate of the Sara Flores Cemetery, the ranchos' constant reminder of the cycle of life.

No Slow Death

José María Reyna has never been afraid of death, only of dying slowly. He told my mother if he ever grew too old or sick to take care of himself, he would end his life rather than face the unfortunate fate of the old: living long enough to become a burden. He knows sooner or later even your own children begin to resent you.

"I've already given myself to God," my grandfather tells his sister Juanita one day as we sit in her front yard watching the cars drive by Sugar Road in Edinburg. "But I hope he sends death when I'm at the rancho, my rancho."

"Porqué en el rancho?" I ask, thinking he will tell me what I have heard him say often: I was born on the rancho, I will die on the rancho.

But what he says is, "I don't want to give my children any more work."

His sister Juanita tells him she has no plans to go back to Mexico. She has nothing left there.

"If I, who am from Mexico, don't go back to see my father and mother's gravesites, much less my children," she tells my grandfather, who is sipping coffee and eating *pan de semita*, a sweet bread, "they'll never go visit me, or bring me flowers." She's already paid Palm Valley Memorial Gardens for her burial plot, just two miles from where we now sit. "It is close by so I won't burden my children," she says before walking inside her house. She walks to the corner room, to the *ropero*, where she keeps her handmade dresses, recuerdos from her dancing days at the senior citizen centers. They are under lock and key until she sells them. She has no plans to wear them again. She returns with a neatly folded shawl made of delicate black and gold thread. It smells of her — musty perfume sprayed many Saturday nights ago. "So you can remember me when I am no longer here," she says, handing it to me.

"I want you to wear it when you bury me," my grandfather tells me. I wrap the rebozo around me. Stretched across my back, it reveals a glittering butterfly.

Questions for Critical Thinking and Writing

1. Hernández writes, "Mexicans are obsessed with death." Why are her family members, in particular, obsessed with death?

2. What does the story about Hernández's grandmother tell you about how she views things like fate and destiny? Nature? Medical science?

3. Explain the significance of *el rancho*. Why is it important for the family to be or not be buried there?

4. **CONNECT TO ANOTHER READING.** In their essays, both Mary Karr (see "The Liars Club," p. 107) and Macarena Hernández recount their childhoods in Texas. In a brief paper, compare the perspectives of Hernández and Karr. Why do you think two women growing up in the same part of the country have such different stories to tell? Do you see any similarities in what they choose to talk about?

ROLANDO HINOJOSA

The novelist and poet Rolando Hinojosa was born in 1929 in Texas's Lower Rio Grande Valley. His works include *Klail City*, *Klail City y sus alrededores*, *Korean Love Songs*, *Mi querido Rafa*, *Los Amigos de Becky*, and *We Happy Few*. He won the esteemed Premio Casa de las Américas Award for *Klail City y sus alrededores*, part of his Klail City Death Trip narratives, comprised of fifteen volumes, and the Quinto Sol Award for Literature for *Estampas del Valle y otras obras*. Hinojosa teaches creative writing at the University of Texas, Austin.

BEFORE YOU READ

In the following poem, Hinojosa explores a particular job that those involved in war must do. What do you know about the details of war, beyond the fighting of battles? How does this poem make war seem more real to someone not involved?

Night Burial Details   *1978*

It's been raining most of the day,
And our dead and their foolish grins
Are still out in the field down there.

The wind is blowing this way, but the stench won't drift over
Until the heat is upon us   5
And them.
And who's to pick up our noble dead?
Ah, the regimental dregs,
The deserters, the cut-and-runners, the awolers, too,
Malingerers all of that screwed up regiment.   10

And so the night passes and with it comes the warm day.
The two and a halves motor in
Laden with canvas bags of the finest, heavy duty, waterproof material
Found anywhere in this man's army.
The hasps are also first-class, rustproof affairs   15
With shiny, yellow plastic tags that are toe bound.
In short, the best canvas bags that sealed bid contracts can buy.
The M.P.'s with side arms and with nothing to do,
Mill around and ponder: just what the hell did *we* do to deserve *this*?
Well, it's join the Army and learn a trade, I say.   20
Just then a chopper hovers over,
But it's waved away:
You're in the wrong territory, chop.

The laws of physics are then observed: Heat rises and with it the diesel fumes,
And the smell of the friendly dead.   25

It matters not to them, of course,
But the Army's made arrangements some forty miles away
For a pit that's half as much again the size of a football field;
Neat as a pin it is and lime-caked, too.
Someone really knows his business there.   30
The job's unfinished here, and now it's starting to rain again.
(It's the season, and you have to expect it.)

As always, rumors are that some of the dregs are officers,
But this is wishful thinking;
Although officers must surely have their private little hells somewhere.   35
This is just a work detail that needs to be done,
And done not your way, not mine, nor anyone else's, save one:
The Army Way: tag and count, tie the bag, the wallets go in that pile there,
And for Chrissakes watch what you're doing!
Out of the wallets dribble the pictures and the condoms, and the money;   40
From the wrists and hands, the watches and the rings,
And out of the pockets, here and there,
A rosary, a GI missal, and a French postcard or two,
Printed in Asia and on the back of which usually reads:
In case of accident, notify the President of the United States,   45
1600 Pennsylvania Avenue. (He's the Commander-in-Chief, don't you know.
At home, it's usually a telegram from the Secretary of Defense who sends
His regards,
And regrets he cannot attend.)

The trucks are now stuffed with close friends,   50
Tighter now than ever, rid of worldly cares,
Each encased, snug and warm, in his private GI womb;
From here they look like so many mail sacks.

Double clutching, the two and a halves manage to get out of the mud;
The drivers are very good at their jobs.   55
One more turn around, and the trucks will form a circle
And head for home in time for the night burial.
The regimental dregs stand guard over the bags,
And the M.P.'s stand guard over them;
They've all earned their pay today.   60
The last truck is finally out;
Its fragile cargo shifts and is shaken up a bit,
But except for shattered nerves,
There are no visible casualties.
And then Hatalski says,   65

    "Give it a rest, Rafe;
    You've been on the binocs all day."

But I wave him off
And now the trucks are rounding the bend,
Lights on, thirty yards apart, all in step, and very proper.   70

    "Take a break, Rafe, and say, Hooker,
    See if you can raise the old man."

"No use, Hat, the trucks've churned up the wire by now.
"Try 'im anyway, we need that right forward ob. bad."

Hook goes through the motions,   75
And I find I need a drink; I check the canteen;
It needs filling and what must be for the very first time,
I take full notice of the Lister bag,
And judge it would do nicely;
Just right, in fact: 80

It too is heavy-duty and waterproof
And of the finest canvas available.
   "No use, Hat; can't get a rise out of HQ."
   "Keep trying, Hook."

And Hook shakes his head,   85
   "Hatalski's becoming Regular Army,
   And he wants us busy."

But that can't be the reason.

Since some of our dead are still down there the trucks'll be back tomorrow.
The M.P.'s, fewer this time, will also be back.   90
Hook'll be at the phone; I'll be at the binocs,
Hatalski will fill shell requisition forms,
And he'll continue to look for our mystery man,
The right forward observer.

Hook says five will get me ten   95
That the dregs will skip early chow now that they know.
Hatalski spits and says,
   "Okay, go down and check the guard."
Hook sets the receiver down and falls in with me
While I go see to the rookies.   100
The rookies are still shaken, but they'll survive this
Although tomorrow they and the dregs and the dead
Will all skip early chow.

QUESTIONS FOR CRITICAL THINKING AND WRITING

1. How does Hinojosa create characters in a poem? How does his method differ from the way you would encounter characters in a work of fiction? Discuss the characters who are burying the dead. Who are they?

2. What details does Hinojosa include about the condition of the corpses? What do those details tell you about the dead men?

3. How does the speaker in the poem feel about his job? About war?

4. **CONNECT TO ANOTHER READING.** In "Night Burial Details" and "Truck" (p. 75), Rolando Hinojosa and Dagoberto Gilb have created characters with a job to do. To what extent do the men share similar backgrounds? How can you tell? Can you assume any similarities in the cultures the men come from? In an essay, compare the speakers in the two works and explain how the authors communicate information about characters. Examine how the approach to character differs in a poem versus a story.

SAM HOUSTON

Samuel Houston (1793–1863), statesman, politician, and soldier, was born in Rockbridge County, Virginia. After the death of his father in 1807, his family moved to Tennessee. In 1809, he ran away from home and lived for some time with a Cherokee tribe that adopted him, referring to him as "Colonneh" or "the Raven." Returning to Tennessee as a young man, Houston was elected to the Tennessee House of Representatives in 1822. He moved to Mexican Texas after being embroiled in a high-profile trial; once there, he took part in military actions following the Texas Declaration of Independence — including participation in the Battle of San Jacinto in 1836. He served as president of the Republic of Texas, was elected a Texas senator after U.S. annexation, and then became governor of the state. The city of Houston bears his name. A staunch unionist, his governorship ended when he refused to swear loyalty to the Southern Confederacy. He died in Huntsville, Texas.

© Bettmann/Corbis.

BEFORE YOU READ

In his Inaugural Address as Governor of Texas, delivered on December 21, 1859, Houston stressed his goal of keeping the early American settlers of Texas safe. What laws do you think would be necessary to protect a fledgling community of Texans? How might Houston have had to address their needs? As you read, keep in mind the main audience for and purpose(s) of this speech. Who is Houston speaking to? What is he trying to persuade his audience to think or do?

From *The Inaugural Address of December 21, 1859*   1879

The subject of our frontier defenses is of absorbing interest. Where it is possible for the Government to give protection to its citizens, it is a duty which cannot be disregarded. The extent of our frontier, stretching as it does, from the Red River to El Paso, on the Rio Grande, and from thence to the mouth of that river, comprises a distance of but little short of two thousand miles. One half of that distance is exposed to Indian depredations, and the other borders upon Mexico, which is in a state of anarchy. Depredations by the Indians are so frequent that to hear of them has almost ceased to excite sympathy and attention in the interior of our State. We have a right to look to the Federal Government for that protection which, as a part of the Confederacy, we are entitled to. The Federal Government has stationed troops on our frontiers, but they are

Infantry, and not calculated for that effective warfare which should be carried on against the Indians, they escape, and the Infantry cannot overtake them. Were a force authorized by the Federal Government of Texan Rangers, who understood the Indian mode of warfare, and whose animals would be capable of subsisting upon prairies, without other forage, the expense would be less to the Government, and their efficiency greater in protecting our frontier, than other description of troops.... We must look beyond mere physical means for defense. There must be a moral influence exerted upon the Indians, and I earnestly hope that will be exerted by the President of the United States, having full confidence in his desire to promote the well-being of the whole country, and that he will not withhold any means in his power to protect our bleeding frontier. The various tribes on our borders, if they were invited to meet at some place convenient on our frontier, and a treaty were made with them to give them a trifling annuity compared to the amount required to afford us but partial protection, would give us peace to our borders. This policy at the time of annexation, gave security to our frontier. Of the future it is fair to judge by the past. In the meantime we must not neglect the demands of emergency; but must ourselves provide means for the immediate defense of our settlements.

Our entire boundary upon the Rio Grande, from the anarchy which prevails in that country, is in an exposed and excited condition. The utter disregard of all law and order in Mexico, has communicated its unhappy influence to this side of the Rio Grande, and a portion of our citizens, at this time, are in a most deplorable condition, and in what it is to eventuate it is impossible to conjecture. The federal arm has been extended there, and I hope will give security and restore tranquility to our people. I will deem it my duty, if sustained by the Legislature, to institute a proper inquiry into the causes which have led to the recent disorders and adopt such measures as will prevent the recurrence of similar outbreaks. I am satisfied they have grown out of local causes, and that no premeditated insurrection was contemplated.

Whilst your representative in the Senate of the United States, being well apprised of the hopeless condition of Mexico, I introduced a measure for the purpose of establishing a Protectorate by the government of the United States over Mexico. The measure was received with disfavor. Aware of the State of Mexican Affairs, I believed the Mexican people utterly incapable of framing a government and maintaining a nationality. This has been demonstrated since their separation from old Spain. Their history is a catalogue of revolutions, of usurpations and oppression. As a neighboring people to us, it is important for the maintainance of good neighborhood, that law and order should exist in that country. The Mexicans are a mild, pastoral and gentle people; and it is only by demagogues and lawless chieftains, who with armed bands have robbed and plundered the people, that the disorders in that country are continued. A guarantee given to these people, for the protection of their lives and property against such, would cause them to rejoice and they would hail with pleasure any measure which might be adopted by any foreign government that would give them peace and security. As a border state, our own security must to a great extent depend upon the condition of things in Mexico, and the restoration of order, and the establishment of good government in that country....

When Texas united her destiny with that of the government of the United States, she took upon herself duties and responsibilities for the faithful performance of which we are pledged as a State. She entered not into the North, nor into the South, but into the Union: her connection was not sectional, but national, and however distinct or diversified her interests may be, as compared with those of other States, she relies upon the same Constitution as they to secure her in the enjoyment of her rights. Making that Constitution the guiding star of our career as a State, let our rivalry be to approximate more closely to it than any of our sister States. It inculcates faithfulness to the Union, let us be faithful to it. Let us, in our relationships with the General government, and with the States of the Confederacy, allow none to excell us in our desires to promote peace and harmony. When our rights are aggressed upon, let us be behind none in repelling attack; but let us be careful to distinguish between the acts of individuals and those of a people, between the wild ravings of fanatics and that public sentiment which truly represents the masses of the people. It is in the diversity of opinion that Democracy may rest securely.

QUESTIONS FOR CRITICAL THINKING AND WRITING

1. Why is Houston, a former soldier, more interested in the authorization of the Texas Rangers than any "official" infantry to protect Texans? What sort of protection did he think they needed that only the Rangers could provide?

2. Why do you think Houston says Mexico is in a "hopeless condition"? Is he speaking of Mexico as a whole? Is he referring to the people, the government, the economy, or something else?

3. How do you understand Houston's call for "a moral influence" to be "exerted upon the Indians"? What do you think he means?

4. CONNECT TO ANOTHER READING. Both Sam Houston and Chief Ten Bears (p. 52) speak with the interests of their people at heart. Compare Houston's address with Ten Bears's speech. Write a short paper explaining how you think each one would view the other. How does each make a case for the security and well-being of his people?

MOLLY IVINS

For a biographical note on Molly Ivins, see page 17.

BEFORE YOU READ

In the following essay, Ivins uses humor to tackle the issue of sexism in her home state of Texas. She writes that sexism is "so deeply ingrained in the culture that it's often difficult to distinguish the disgusting from the outrageous or the offensive from the amusing." Can sexism ever be a good thing, as she suggests? Does it make women stronger? What does Ivins believe about the behavior of men and women in Texas? Do her ideas, expressed in this essay in 1986, hold up more than twenty years later?

Is Texas America? 1986

They used to say that Texas was hell on women and horses — I don't know why they stopped. Surely not because much of the citizenry has had its consciousness raised, as they say in the jargon of the women's movement, on the issue of sexism. Just a few months ago one of our state representatives felt moved to compare women and horses — it was the similarity he wanted to emphasize. Of course some Texas legislator can be found to say any fool thing, but this guy's comments met with general agreement from his colleagues. One can always dismiss the entire Legislature as a particularly deplorable set of Texans, but as Sen. Carl Parker observes, if you took all the fools out of the Lege, it wouldn't be a representative body anymore.

I should confess that I've always been more of an observer than a participant in Texas Womanhood: The spirit was willing but I was declared ineligible on grounds of size early. You can't be six feet tall and cute, both. I think I was first named captain of the basketball team when I was four and that's what I've been ever since. I spent my girlhood as a Clydesdale among thoroughbreds. I clopped along amongst them cheerfully, admiring their grace, but the strange training rituals they went through left me secretly relieved that no one would ever expect me to step on a racetrack. I think it is quite possible to grow up in Texas as an utter failure in flirting, gentility, cheerleading, sexpottery, and manipulation and still be without any permanent scars. Except one. We'd all rather be blonde.

Please understand I'm not whining when I point out that Texas sexism is of an especially rank and noxious variety — this is more a Texas brag. It is my belief that it is virulence of Texas sexism that accounts for the strength of Texas women. It's what we have to overcome that makes us formidable survivors, say I with some complacency.

As has been noted elsewhere, there are several strains of Texan culture: They are all rotten for women. There is the Southern belle nonsense of our Confederate heritage, that little-woman-on-a-pedestal, flirtatious, "you're so cute when you're mad," Scarlett O'Hara myth that leads, quite naturally, to the equally pernicious legend of the Iron Magnolia. Then there's the machismo of our Latin heritage, which affects not only our Chicana sisters, but has been integrated into Texas culture quite as thoroughly as barbecue, rodeo, and Tex-Mex food.

Next up is the pervasive good-ol'-boyism of the *Redneckus texensis*, that remarkable tribe that has made the pickup truck with the gun rack across the back window and the beer cans flying out the window a synonym for Texans worldwide. Country music is a good place to investigate and find reflected the attitudes of kickers toward women (never ask what a kicker kicks). It's your basic, familiar virgin/whore dichotomy — either your "Good-Hearted Woman" or "Your Cheatin' Heart," with the emphasis on the honky-tonk angels. Nor is the jock idolatry that permeates the state helpful to our gender: Football is not a game here, it's a matter of blood and death. Woman's role in the state's national game is limited, significantly, to cheerleading. In this regard, I can say with great confidence that Texas changeth not — the hopelessly intense, heart-breaking longing with which most Texas girls still want to be cheerleader can be observed at every high school, every September.

Last but not least in the litany of cultures that help make the lives of Texas women so challenging is the legacy of the frontier — not the frontier that Texas women lived on, but the one John Wayne lived on. Anyone who knows the real history of the frontier knows it is a saga of the strength of women. They worked as hard as men, they fought as hard as men, they suffered as much as men. But in the cowboy movies that most contemporary Texans grew up on, the big, strong man always protects "the little lady" or "the gals" from whatever peril threatens. Such nonsense. Mary Ann Goodnight was often left alone at the JA Ranch near the Palo Duro Canyon. One day in 1877, a cowboy rode into her camp with three chickens in a sack as a present for her. He naturally expected her to cook and eat the fowl, but Goodnight kept them as pets. She wrote in her diary, "No one can ever know how much company they were." Life for farm and ranch wives didn't improve much over the next 100 years. Ruth White raised nine children on a farm near High, Texas, in the 1920s and thirties. She used to say, "Everything on this farm is either hungry or heavy."

All of these strains lead to a form of sexism so deeply ingrained in the culture that it's often difficult to distinguish the disgusting from the outrageous or the offensive from the amusing. One not infrequently sees cars or trucks sporting the bumper sticker HAVE FUN — BEAT THE HELL OUT OF SOMEONE YOU LOVE. Another is: IF YOU LOVE SOMETHING, SET IT FREE. IF IT DOESN'T COME BACK, TRACK IT DOWN AND KILL IT. I once heard a legislator order a lobbyist, "Get me two sweathogs for tonight." At a benefit "roast" for the battered women's shelter in El Paso early in 1985, a couple of the male politicians told rape jokes to amuse the crowd. Most Texas sexism is not intended to be offensive — it's entirely unconscious. A colleague of mine was touring the new death chamber in Huntsville last year with a group of other reporters. Their guide called to warn those inside they were coming through, saying, "I'm coming over with eight reporters and one woman." Stuff like that happens to you four or five times a day for long enough, it will wear you down some.

Other forms of the phenomenon are, of course, less delightsome. Women everywhere are victims of violence with depressing regularity. Texas is a more violent place than most of the rest of America, for reasons having to do with guns, machismo, frontier traditions, and the heterogeneous population. While the law theoretically applies to male and female alike, by unspoken convention, a man who offs his wife or girlfriend is seldom charged with murder one: we wind up filed under the misnomer manslaughter.

That's the bad news for Texas women — the good news is that all this adversity has certainly made us a bodacious bunch of overcomers. And rather pleasant as a group, I always think, since having a sense of humor about men is not a luxury here; it's a necessity. The feminists often carry on about the importance of role models and how little girls need positive role models. When I was a kid, my choice of Texas role models went from Ma Ferguson to the Kilgore Rangerettes. Of course I wanted to be Rangerette: Ever seen a picture of Ma? Not that we haven't got real women heroes, of course, just that we were never taught anything about them. You used to have to take Texas history two or three times in order to get a high school diploma in this state: The Yellow Rose of Texas and Belle Starr were the only women in our history books. Kaye Northcott notes that all the big cities in the state have men's last names — Houston, Austin, Dallas. All women got was some small towns called after

The Outlaw Belle Starr. Born Myra Belle Shirley, Belle Starr (1848–1889) was first introduced to the outlaw life when the James-Younger Gang sought refuge in her Texas home. Following this acquaintance, Belle pursued the criminal life as well as several love affairs with other outlaws. One year prior to her death, she said, "I regard myself as a woman who has seen much of life." The mystery of her murder has yet to be solved. In this photo, taken circa 1870, Starr holds a gun in one hand and carries a second in the holster at her waist.
© Getty Images.

their front names: Alice, Electra, Marfa. This is probably because, as Eleanor Brackenridge of San Antonio (1837–1924) so elegantly put it, "Foolish modesty lags behind while brazen impudence goes forth and eats the pudding." Brackenridge did her part to correct the lag by founding the Texas Woman Suffrage Association in 1913.

It is astonishing how recently Texas women have achieved equal legal rights. I guess you could say we made steady progress even before we could vote — the state did raise the age of consent for a woman from 7 to 10 in 1890 — but it went a little smoother after we got some say in it. Until June 26, 1918, all Texans could vote except "idiots, imbeciles, aliens, the insane, and women." The battle over woman's suffrage in Texas was long and fierce. Contempt and ridicule were the favored weapons against women. Women earned the right to vote through years of struggle; the precious victory was not something handed to us by generous men. From that struggle emerged a generation of Texas women whose political skills and leadership abilities have affected Texas politics for decades. Even so, Texas women were not permitted to serve on juries until 1954. As late as 1969, married women did not have full property rights. And until 1972, under Article 1220 of the Texas Penal Code, a man could murder his wife and her lover if he found them "in a compromising position" and get away with it as "justifiable homicide." Women, you understand, did not have equal shooting rights. Although Texas was one of the first states to ratify the Equal Rights Amendment, which has been part of the Texas Constitution since 1972, we continue to work for fairer laws concerning problems such as divorce, rape, child custody, and access to credit.

Texas women are just as divided by race, class, age, and educational level as are other varieties of human beings. There's a pat description of "what every Texas woman wants" that varies a bit from city to city, but the formula that Dallas females have been labeled with goes something like this: "Be a Pi Phi at Texas or SMU, marry a man who'll buy you a house in Highland Park, hold the wedding at Highland Park Methodist (flowers by Kendall Bailey), join the Junior League, send the kids to St. Mark's and Hockaday in the winter and Camps Longhorn and Waldemar in the summer, plus cotillion lessons at the Dallas Country Club, have an unlimited charge account at Neiman's as a birthright but buy almost all your clothes at Highland Park Village from Harold's or the Polo Shop, get your hair done at Paul Neinast's or Lou's and drive a Jeep Wagoneer for carpooling and a Mercedes for fun." There is a kicker equivalent of this scenario that starts, "Every Texas girl's dream is a double-wide in a Lubbock trailer park. . . ." But I personally believe it is unwise ever to be funny at the expense of kicker women. I once met a kicker lady who was wearing a blouse of such a vivid pink you could close your eyes and still see the color; this confection was perked up with some big rhinestone buttons and a lot of ruffles across an impressive bosom. "My," said I, "where did you get that blouse?" She gave me a level look and drawled. "Honey, it come from mah coutouri-ay, Jay Cee Penn-ay." And if that ain't class, you can kiss my grits.

To my partisan eye, it seems that Texas women are more animated and friendly than those from, say, Nebraska. I suspect this comes from early training: Girls in Texas high schools are expected to walk through the halls smiling and saying "Hi" to everyone they meet. Being enthusiastic is bred into us, as is a certain amount of obligatory social hypocrisy stemming from the Southern tradition of manners, which does rather tend to emphasize pleasantness more than honesty in social situations. Many Texas women have an odd greeting call — when they haven't seen a good friend for a long time, the first glimpse will provoke the cry, "Ooooooo-honey, how good to see yew again!" It sounds sort of like the "Sooooooey, pig" call.

Mostly Texas women are tough in some very fundamental ways. Not unfeminine, nor necessarily unladylike, just tough. It may be possible for a little girl to grow to womanhood in this state entirely sheltered from the rampant sexism all around her — but it's damned difficult. The result is that Texas women tend to know how to cope. We can cope with put-downs and come-ons, with preachers and hustlers, with drunks and cowboys. And when it's all over, if we stick together and work, we'll come out better than the sister who's buried in a grave near Marble Falls under a stone that says, "Rudolph Richter, 1822–1915, and Wife."

Questions for Critical Thinking and Writing

1. For her thesis, Ivins writes, "It is virulence of Texas sexism that accounts for the strength of Texas women." Do you think she makes a case that backs up this claim? Why or why not?

2. What are the two different "legacies of the frontier"? What effect does each one have on Texas women?

3. Ivins says Texas sexism is "not intended to be offensive." What does she mean by that?

4. **CONNECT TO ANOTHER READING.** In their essays, Molly Ivins and Gloria Anzaldúa (see p. 37) both discuss the hardships women living in Texas face; both mention the problem of violence against women. Write an essay comparing how each writer treats this material. Consider Ivins's and Anzaldúa's examples and any stylistic differences. Feel free to discuss the authors' backgrounds if it helps explain why they make the choices they do.

Barbara Jordan

Texas Congresswoman Barbara Charline Jordan (1936–1996) was born in Houston's Fifth Ward. As an African American coming of age in the 1950s, she experienced segregation and discrimination firsthand. Jordan, who graduated from Texas Southern University in 1956 and from Boston University Law School in 1959, became the first African American state senator in Texas and the first African American from a southern state to serve in the U.S. House of Representatives. During the U.S. House of Representatives Judiciary Committee's Watergate hearings, she received national exposure when she gave televised speeches supporting the impeachment of President Richard Nixon. Jordan spoke of her role in the Watergate hearings, referring to the preamble to the Constitution: "When that document was completed, on the seventeenth of September in 1787, I was not included in that 'We, the people.' I felt somehow for many years that

Barbara Jordan. Senator Jordan gives the keynote speech at the 1992 Democratic National Convention.
© Bettmann/Corbis.

George Washington and Alexander Hamilton just left me out by mistake. But through the process of amendment, interpretation, and court decision I have finally been included in 'We, the people.'" Jordan delivered a keynote address at the Democratic National Convention in 1976, when Jimmy Carter was nominated, and then again in 1992, when Bill Clinton was elected. Jordan was awarded the Presidential Medal of Freedom in 1994.

BEFORE YOU READ

Throughout her political career, Jordan was concerned with fairness and equality in the political, social, and economic spheres of the United States. Given the 2008 election of Barack Obama, do you think the discrepancies Jordan wanted to see disappear are still in place? Do you believe this country is ready to elect a woman president? Why or why not?

From *The Keynote Address to the Democratic National Convention, July 13, 1992*

When the economy is growing and we are treating our air, water and soil kindly, all of us prosper. We all benefit from economic expansion. I certainly do not mean the thinly disguised racism and elitism of some kind of trickle down economics. I mean an economy where a young black woman or man from the Fifth Ward in Houston or south-central Los Angeles, or a young person in the *colonias* of the lower Rio Grande valley, can attend public schools and learn the skills that will enable her or him to prosper. We must have an economy that does not force the migrant worker's child to miss school in order to earn less than the minimum wage just so the family can have one meal a day. That is the moral bankruptcy that trickle down economics is all about. We can change the direction of America's economic engine and become proud and competitive again. The American dream is not dead. True, it is gasping for breath but it is not dead. However, there is no time to waste because the American Dream is slipping away from too many. It is slipping away from too many black and brown mothers and their children; from the homeless of every color and sex; from the immigrants living in communities without water and sewer systems. The American Dream is slipping away from the workers whose jobs are no longer there because we are better at building war equipment that sits in warehouses than we are at building decent housing; from the workers on indefinite layoffs while their chief executive officers are making bonuses that are more than the worker will take home in 10 or 20 or 30 years. . . .

One overdue change already underway is the number of women challenging the councils of political power dominated by white-male policy makers. That horizon is limitless. What we see today is simply a dress rehearsal for the day and time we meet in convention to nominate . . . Madame President. This country can ill afford to continue to function using less than half of its human resources, brain power and kinetic energy. Our 19th century visitor from France, de Tocqueville, observed in his work *Democracy in America*, "If I were asked to what singular substance do I mainly attribute the prosperity and growing strength of the American people, I should reply: To the superiority of their women." The 20th century will not close without our presence being keenly felt. . . .

QUESTIONS FOR CRITICAL THINKING AND WRITING

1. Based on this passage, what do you think Jordan means by the eighties term *"trickle down economics"*?

2. Jordan refers to the "American Dream," saying, "it is gasping for breath, but it is not dead." What is the American Dream? What purpose does it serve?

3. Is it controversial for Jordan to suggest the nomination of "Madame President" at the 1992 Democratic National Convention? Why or why not?

4. In an essay, provide an analysis of Jordan's remarks to the 1992 Democratic National Convention. What are the main points of her argument? How does she support these points? Overall, how effective is her speech in terms of persuasiveness? Alternately, you may wish to compare or contrast Jordan's speech to those made in other public speeches included in this anthology: speeches by Chief Ten Bears (p. 52) or Sam Houston (p. 97).

MARY KARR

Mary Karr — poet, essayist, and memoirist — was born in 1955 in Groves, Texas. Her memoir *The Liars' Club* became a bestseller in 1995 and was followed by another memoir, *Cherry*, in 2000. Among the influences on her writing, Karr points to African American poet Etheridge Knight. Karr has won both a Guggenheim Fellowship and Pushcart Prizes for her poems and essays and holds an MFA from Goddard College, where she studied with fiction writer Tobias Wolff. She is the Peck Professor of English Literature at Syracuse University.

BEFORE YOU READ

Karr's memoir chronicles her childhood in southeast Texas; in this section, she recounts witnessing her father's struggles with debt. What does this passage say about life in Texas in 1961? What can you tell about the town in which Karr grew up?

From *The Liars' Club:* Texas 1961   *1995*

Grandma wound up leaving Mother a big pile of money, which didn't do us a lick of good, though Lord knows we needed it. Daddy's strike had dragged on till mid-March, pulling us way down in our bill-paying. He managed to keep up with the mortgage and utilities okay, but the grocery and drug bills and other sundries got out from under him. When he picked up his check at the paymaster's window on Fridays, he cashed it right there. Then he'd drive to Leechfield Pharmacy and go straight up to the pill counter in back to tell Mr. Juarez — kids called him Bugsy, after the cartoon bunny — that he'd come to pay at his bill. I can still see Daddy winking while he said it, *at.* He'd squint down at his billfold and lick his thumb and make a show of picking out a single crisp five-dollar bill and squaring it up on the counter between them. But that little "at" held back a whole tide of shame. It implied the bill weighed more than Daddy, superseded him in a way. In Jasper County, where he'd been raised, buying on credit was a sure sign of a man overreaching what he was. Even car loans were unheard-of, and folks were known to set down whole laundry sacks stuffed with one-dollar bills when it came time to pick up a new Jeep or tractor.

Bugsy knew these things. They mattered to him. He was a kind guy, prone to giving me comic books for free because it tickled him that I read so well. He always acted like he hated to take Daddy's money when it slid his way. "Heck, Pete. Put that back. We weren't a-waiting on this," he'd say, and Daddy would slide the bill closer and tell him to go on and take it. Then Bugsy would shrug out an okay. He'd ring some zeros up on the cash register and slip the bill into the right stack. He kept his accounts in a green book under the counter. He'd haul that out, find Daddy's name with his thick nicotine-stained finger, and note down the payment. Before we left, Bugsy usually led me to the back office, where he'd draw out his pocket knife to cut the binding cord on the new stack of funny books invariably standing in the corner. I'd sit on his desk and read out loud an entire issue of *Superman* or *Archie*, which skill caused him to smile into his coffee mug. Daddy would shake his head at this and say that I didn't need egging on because I had already gotten too big for my britches as it was.

That was the dance we went through with Bugsy on payday. The movements of it were both so exact and so fiercely casual that I never for a minute doubted that this whole money thing was, in fact, not casual at all, but serious as a stone. All the rest of the week, nobody talked about it. That silence slid over our house like a cold iron. But woe be it to you if you didn't finish your bowl of black-eyed peas, or if you failed to shut the icebox door flush so that it leaked cold and thereby ran up the electric. Daddy would come up behind you and shove that door all the way to or scoop the last peas into his own mouth with your very spoon. After doing so, he'd stare at you from the side of his face as if holding down a wealth of pissed-off over your evil wastefulness.

Evenings he wasn't working, he sat in bed to study his receipts and bills. He liked to spread out the old ones stamped PAID along the left side of the bedcovers. The new statements still in their envelopes ran along the right. He'd worked out a whole ritual to handle those bills. When one hit the mailbox, he slit it open, then marked down what he owed over the front address window where his name showed through. That way he sort of nodded at the debt right off, like he was saying *I know, I know*. Plus, he then didn't have to reopen and unfold every bill in order to worry over it. With all those envelopes staggered out in front of him, he drew hard on bottle after bottle of Lone Star beer and ciphered what he owed down the long margins of *The Leechfield Gazette*, all the time not saying boo about one dime of it.

I knew full well that people had way bigger problems than those Daddy had. Lots of guys didn't have jobs and houses at all. Or they had kids fall slobbering sick with leukemia, not to mention the umpteen-zillion people who were born in the Kalahari Desert or the streets of Calcutta blind or missing limbs or half-rotted-up as lepers. But Daddy's nightly cipherings were the most concentrated form of worry I've ever witnessed up close. That long line of numbers, done in his slanty, spidery scrawl, was not unlike the prayer that the penitent says over and over so that either the hope of that prayer or the full misery of what it's supposed to stave off will finally sink in.

QUESTIONS FOR CRITICAL THINKING AND WRITING

1. Does Bugsy need the money Karr's father gives him? What do her descriptions of Bugsy and her father tell you about their character?

2. Karr's father seems nonchalant about the money he owes when he goes to Bugsy's store. At what point in the section can you tell he is worried about money?

3. What does Karr's family have in common with people from other poor countries (for example, the people of the Kalahari Desert or Calcutta, to whom she refers at the end of this passage)? How is her situation unique to America, or Texas?

LARRY McMURTRY

Larry Jeff McMurtry was born in 1936 in Wichita Falls, Texas. The ranch in Archer County, Texas, where he spent his childhood, is the place on which he bases his fictional town, Thalia. McMurtry has said of his home: "I can't escape it in my fiction. I can work away from it, but I always start here." His works, usually based in the West, and in Texas in particular, include *The Last Picture Show* (the novel from which the following excerpt is taken); *Horseman, Pass By*; *All My Friends Are Going to Be Strangers*; *Terms of Endearment*; *Cadillac Jack*; *Texasville*; *Lonesome Dove*; and *Buffalo Girls*. Many of his works, including *The Last Picture Show*, have been adapted for film. McMurtry won a Pulitzer Prize for *Lonesome Dove*; in 2006 he won (with Diana Ossana) the Academy Award for Best Adapted Screenplay for the film *Brokeback Mountain*, which was based on a short story by E. Annie Proulx.

BEFORE YOU READ

McMurtry's story follows two boys as they cross from Texas into Mexico and back again. What are some of the differences between Thalia, Texas, and Matamoros, Mexico? What sort of culture shock do the boys experience? How does the trip to Mexico affect them — and why?

From *The Last Picture Show*   1966

All day the boys alternated, one driving the other sleeping, and by late evening they were in the Valley, driving between the green orange groves. It was amazing how different the world was, once the plains were left behind. In the Valley there were even palm trees. The sky was violet, and dusk lingered until they were almost to Matamoros. Every few miles they passed roadside groceries, lit with yellow light bulbs and crowded with tables piled high with corn and squash, cabbages and tomatoes.

"This is a crazy place," Duane said. "Who you reckon eats all that squash?"

They drove straight on through Brownsville and paid a fat, bored toll-house keeper twenty cents so they could drive across the bridge. Below them was the Rio Grande, a river they had heard about all their lives. Its waters were mostly dark, touched only here and there by the yellow bridge lights. Several Mexican boys in ragged shirts were sitting on one of the guardrails, spitting into the water and chattering to one another.

A few blocks from the bridge they came to a stoplight on a pole, with four or five boys squatting by it. Apparently someone had run into the light pole because it was leaning away from the street at a forty-five degree angle. As soon as Sonny stopped one of the boys ran out and jumped lightly onto the running board.

"Girl?" he said. "Boy's Town? Dirty movie?"

"Well, I guess," Sonny said. "I guess," Sonny said. "I guess that's what we came for."

The boy quickly got in the cab and began to chatter directions in Tex-Mex — Sonny followed them as best he could. They soon left the boulevard and got into some of the narrowest streets the boys had ever seen. Barefooted kids and cats and dogs were playing in the street, night or no night, and they moved aside for the pickup very reluctantly. A smell of onions seemed to pervade the whole town, and the streets went every which direction. There were lots of intersections but no stop signs — apparently the right of way belonged to the driver with the most nerve. Sonny kept stopping at the intersections, but that was a reversal of local custom: most drivers beeped their horns and speeded up, hoping to dart through before anyone could hit them.

Mexico was more different from Thalia than either of the boys would have believed. The number of people who went about at night was amazing to them. In Thalia three or four boys on the courthouse square constituted a lively crowd, but the streets of Matamoros teemed with people. Groups of men stood on what, in Thalia, would have been sidewalks, children rushed about in the dust, and old men sat against buildings.

Their guide finally ordered them to stop in front of a dark lump that was apparently some sort of dwelling.

"This couldn't be no whorehouse," Duane said. "It ain't big enough to have a whore in it."

Not knowing what else to do, they got out and followed their guide to the door. A paunchy Mexican in his undershirt and khakis opened it and grunted at the guide. "Ees got movies," the boy said.

They all went inside, into a bedroom. Through an open doorway the boys could see an old woman stirring something in a pot, onions and tomatoes it smelled like. An old man with no shirt on and white hair on his chest sat at a table staring at some dominoes. Neither the old man nor old woman so much as glanced at the boys. There were two beds in the bedroom and on one of them three little Mexican boys were curled up, asleep. Sonny felt strange when he saw them. They looked very helpless, and he could not feel it was very polite for Duane and him to barge into their room. The paunchy man immediately brought up the subject of movies. "Ten dollars," he said. "Got all kinds."

He knelt and drew a tiny little projector out from under the bed and took several rolls of eight-millimeter film out of a little bureau. The boys looked uncomfortably at one another. They either had to pay and watch the movies or else refuse and leave, and since they had driven five hundred miles to see some wickedness it was pointless to refuse. Duane handed over a ten dollar bill and the man stuffed it in his pocket and calmly began to clear one of the beds. He picked the sleeping boys up one at a time, carried them into the kitchen, and deposited them under the table where the old man sat. The little boys moaned a little and stirred in their sleep, but they didn't wake up. The paunchy man then put the projector on their bed and prepared to show the movies on a sheet hung against the opposite wall.

"I don't like this," Sonny said, appalled. "I never come all this way just to get some kids out of bed. If he ain't got a better place than this to show them I'd just as soon go on."

Duane was of the same mind, but when they tried to explain themselves, the guide and the projectionist both seemed puzzled.

"Ees okay," the guide said. "Sleepin' away." He gestured at the three little boys, all of whom were sound asleep on the dirt floor.

Sonny and Duane were stubborn. Even though the little boys were asleep, it wouldn't do: they couldn't enjoy a dirty movie so long as they were in sight of the displaced kids. Finally the projectionist shrugged, picked up the projector, and led them back through the hot kitchen and across an alley. The guide followed, carrying the film. Above them the sky was dark and the stars very bright.

They came to what seemed to be a sort of long outhouse, and when the guide knocked a thin, middle-aged man opened the door. He had only one leg, but no crutch, the room being so small that he could easily hop from one resting place to the next. As soon as they were all inside the guide informed the boys that it would cost them five dollars more because of the change of rooms: the one-legged man could not be put to the trouble of sitting through a pornographic movie for nothing. Sonny paid it and the projectionist plugged the projector into a light socket. An old American calendar hung on the door, a picture of a girl in mechanic's overalls on the front of it. The one-legged man simply turned the calendar around and they had a screen.

"You mean they're going to show it on the back of a calendar," Duane said. "For fifteen dollars?"

The light was turned off and the projector began to buzz — the title of the picture was *Man's Best Friend*. It was clearly an old picture, because the lady who came on the screen was dressed like ladies in Laurel and Hardy movies. The similarity was so strong that for a moment the boys expected Laurel and Hardy to come on the screen and do dirty things to her. As the plot unfolded the print became more and more scratchy and more and more faded; soon it was barely possible to tell that the figures on the screen were human. The boys leaned forward to get a better look and were amazed to discover that the figures on the screen *weren't* all human. One of the actors was a German shepherd dog.

"My God," Duane said.

They both immediately felt the trip was worthwhile, if only for the gossip value. Nobody in Thalia had ever seen a dog and a lady behaving that way: clearly it was the ultimate depravity, even more depraved than having congress with Negro whores. They were speechless. A man came on and replaced the dog, and then the dog came back on and he and the man teamed up. The projectionist and the guide chuckled with delight at this development, but the boys were too surprised to do anything but watch. The ugliness of it all held them spellbound. When it was over they walked to the pickup in silence, followed by the guide and the projectionist. The latter was making a sales pitch.

"Lots more reels," he said. "Got French, Gypsy, Chinese lesbian, all kinds. Five dollars a reel from now on."

The boys shook their heads. They wanted to get away and think. The guide shrugged and climbed in beside them and they drove away, leaving the fat man in the middle of the road.

"I hope he puts them kids back in bed," Sonny commented.

"Boy's Town now," the guide said happily. "Five hundred girls there. Clean, too."

They soon left the downtown area and bumped off toward the outskirts of Matamoros. A red Chevrolet with Texas license plates was just in front of them, throwing the white dust of the dirt road up into their headlights. Soon they saw Boy's Town, the neon lights from the larger cabarets winking red and green against the night. At first it looked like there were a hundred clubs, but after they drove around a while they saw that there were only fifteen or twenty big places, one on every corner. Between the corners were dark, unlit rows of cribs. The guide gestured contemptuously at the cribs and took them to a place called the Cabaret ZeeZee. When the boys parked, a fat policeman in khakis walked up and offered to open the door for them, but the guide chattered insultingly to him and he shrugged lazily and turned away.

The boys entered the cabaret timidly, expecting to be mobbed at once by whores or else slugged by Mexican gangsters, but neither thing happened. They were simply ignored. There was a large jukebox and a few couples dancing, but most of the people in the club were American boys, sitting around tables.

"The competition's gonna be worse here than it is in Thalia," Duane said. "We might as well get some beer."

They sat down at one of the tile-topped tables and waited several minutes before a waitress came over and got their order. She brought them the first Mexican beer they had ever tasted, and they drank the first bottles thirstily. In their tired, excited state the beer quickly took effect—before they knew it they had had five bottles apiece, and the fatigue of the trip seemed to be dropping away. A fat-faced girl in a green blouse came over, introduced herself as Juanita, and with no further preamble squeezed Sonny intimately through his blue jeans. He was amazed. Though responsive, he felt the evening would bring better things than Juanita, so he politely demurred. Juanita went around and squeezed Duane the same way, but got the same reply.

"Texas ees full of queers," she said, swishing her buttocks derogatorily as she walked away. The boys contemplated themselves over the beer bottles, wondering if they had been seriously insulted.

As the night wore on Sonny gradually set his mind on a slim, black-headed girl who spent most of her time on the dance floor, dancing with boys from Texas A & M. There were a good many boys from Texas A & M in the cabaret.

"I thought Aggies was all irresistible cocksmen," Duane said. "What's so many of them doing in a whorehouse?"

In time Sonny approached the girl, whose name was Maria. She cheerfully came to the table with him and downed three whiskeys while he was having a final beer. Between drinks she blew her warm, slightly sticky breath in his ear and squeezed him the way Juanita had.

"All night party?" she asked. "Jus' tweenty-five dollars. We can leef right now."

It seemed ungallant to haggle with such a confident girl, so Sonny agreed. It turned out he owed eight dollars for the drinks, but it didn't seem gallant to haggle about that either. He paid, and Maria led him out the back door of the Cabaret ZeeZee into a very dark alley, where the only light was from the bright stars far above. The place she took him didn't even have a door, just a blue curtain with a light behind it. The room was extremely tiny. The one light bulb was in a socket on the wall and the bed was an old iron cot with a small mattress and a thin green bedspread.

In the room, Maria seemed less perky than she had in the club. She looked younger than she had inside. Sonny watched her unzip her dress—her back was brown and smooth, but when she turned to face him he was really surprised. Her breasts were heavy, her nipples large and purplish, and she was clearly pregnant. He had never seen a pregnant woman naked before, but he knew from the heavy bulge of her abdomen that she must be carrying a child. She tried to look at him with whorish gaiety, but somehow it didn't work: the smile was without life, and showed her gums. When he was undressed she splashed him with coolish water from a brown pitcher, and scrutinized him with such care that an old worry popped into his mind. Perhaps his equipment was too small? He had worried about that when he first began to go with Ruth, and had even tried to find out how large one's equipment was supposed to be, but the only two reference works in the high-school library were the *World Book* and the *Texas Almanac*, neither of which had anything helpful on penises. Gradually it had ceased to worry him, but with Maria he had begun to feel generally hesitant.

"But aren't you going to have a baby?" he asked, not sure that the question was proper.

Maria nodded. "Two already," she said, meaning to reassure him. Her heavy breasts and large grape-colored nipples were not at all congruous with her thin calves and girlish shoulders.

Sonny lay down with her on the cot, but he knew even before he began that somehow twenty-five dollars had been lost. He didn't want to stay in the room all night, or even very much of it.

Two minutes later it came home to him why Ruth had insisted they make love on the floor: the cot springs wailed and screamed, and the sound made him feel as though every move he made was sinful. He had driven five hundred miles to get away from Thalia, and the springs took him right back, made him feel exposed. Everyone in town would know that he had done it with a pregnant whore. Suddenly he ceased to care about the twenty-five dollars, or about anything; the fatigues of the long trip, down from the plains, through the hill country and the brush country, through Austin and San Antone, five hundred miles of it all pressed against the backs of his legs and up his body, too heavy to support. To Maria's amazement he simply stopped and went to sleep.

When he awoke, he was very hot. The green counterpane was soaked with his sweat. It was not until he had been awake a minute or two that he realized the sun was shining in his face. He was still in the room where Maria had brought him, but the room had no roof—the night before he had not even noticed. It was just an open crib.

He hurriedly got up and put on his clothes, his head aching. While he was tying his shoes he suddenly had to vomit, and barely made it past the blue curtain into the street. When he had finished vomiting and was kneeling in the white dust waiting for his strength to come back he heard a slow clop-clop and looked up to see a strange wagon rounding the corner into his part of the street. It was a water wagon, drawn by a decrepit brown mule and driven by an old man. The wagon was entirely filled by a large rubber water tank wrapped in ragged canvas; as the wagon moved the water sloshed out of the open tank and dripped down the sides of the wagon into the white dust. The old man wore a straw hat so old that it had turned brown. His grizzled whiskers were as white as Sam the Lion's hair. As he stopped the mule, three or four whores stepped out of their cribs with water pitchers in their hands. One passed right by Sonny, a heavy woman with a relaxed face and large white breasts that almost spilled out of her green robe. The whores were barefooted and seemed much happier than they had seemed the night before. They chattered like high-school girls and came lightly to the wagon to get their water. The old man spoke to them cheerfully, and when the first group had filled their pitchers he popped the mule lightly with the rein and proceeded up the street, the slow clop-clop of the mule's feet very loud in the still morning. When he passed where Sonny was kneeling the old man nodded to him kindly and gestured with a tin dipper he had in his hand. Sonny gratefully took a dipper of water from him, using it to wash the sour taste out of his mouth. The old man smiled at him sympathetically and said something in a philosophic tone, something which Sonny took to mean that life was a matter of ups and downs. He stayed where he was and watched the wagon until it rounded the next corner. As it moved slowly up the street the whores of Matamoros came out of their cribs, some of them combing their black hair, some with white bosoms uncovered, all with brown pitchers in their hands and coins for the old waterman.

Sonny found Duane asleep in the front seat of the pickup, his legs sticking out the window. Three little boys were playing in the road, trying to lead a dusty white goat across into a pasture of scraggly mesquite. The goat apparently wanted to go into the Cabaret ZeeZee. A depressed looking spotted dog followed behind the boys and occasionally yapped discouragedly at the goat.

Duane was too bleary and sick to do more than grunt. His hair was plastered to his temples with sweat. "You drive," he said.

By some miracle Sonny managed to wind his way through Matamoros to the Rio Grande — in daylight the water in the river was green. The boys stood groggily under the custom's shed for a few minutes, wondering why in the world they had been so foolish as to come all the way to Mexico. Thalia seemed an impossible distance away.

"I don't know if I can make it," Sonny said. "How much money we got?"

They found, to their dismay, that their money had somehow evaporated. They had four dollars between them. There was the money that Sam and Genevieve had given them, hidden in the seat springs, but they had not planned to use that.

"I guess we can pay them back in a week or two," Sonny said. "We'll have to use it."

When the customs men were through the boys got back in the pickup and drove slowly out of Brownsville, along the Valley highway. Heat waves shimmered above the green cabbage fields. Despite the sun and heat Duane soon went to sleep again and slept heavily, wallowing in his own sweat. Sonny drove automatically; he was depressed, but not exactly sleepy, and he paced himself from town to town, not daring to think any farther ahead than the next city limits sign.

Soon the thought of Ruth began to bother him. In retrospect it seemed incredibly foolish that he should drive a thousand miles to go to sleep on a pregnant girl's stomach, when any afternoon he could have a much better time with Ruth. The thought of her slim, familiar body and cool hands suddenly made him very horny and even more depressed with himself. It occurred to him that he might even be diseased, and he stopped in a filling station in Alice to inspect himself. Duane woke up and exhibited similar anxieties. For the rest of the day they stopped and peed every fifty miles, just to be sure they could.

There was money enough for gas, but not much for food, so they managed on Cokes, peanuts, and a couple of candy bars. Evening finally came, coolness with it, and the boys got a second wind. The trip ceased to seem like such a fiasco: after all, they had been to Mexico, visited whorehouses, seen dirty movies. In Thalia it would be regarded as a great adventure, and they could hardly wait to tell about it. The country around Thalia had never looked so good to them as it did when they came back into it, at four in the morning. The dark pastures, the farmhouses, the oil derricks and even the jackrabbits that went dashing across the road in front of them, all seemed comfortable, familiar, private even, part of what was theirs and no one else's. After the strangeness of Matamoros the lights of Thalia were especially reassuring.

Duane was driving when they pulled in. He whipped through the red light and turned toward the café. Genevieve would be glad to see they were safely back.

To their astonishment, the café was dark. No one at all was there. The café had never been closed, not even on Christmas, and the boys were stunned. Inside, one little light behind the counter shone on the aspirin, the cough-drops, the chewing gum, and cheap cigars.

"It ain't a holiday, is it?" Sonny said.

There was nothing to do but go over to the courthouse and wake up Andy Fanner — he would know what had happened.

Andy woke up hard, but they kept at him and he finally got out of the car and rubbed his stubbly jaw, trying to figure out what the boys wanted.

"Oh yeah, you all been gone, ain't you," he said. "Gone to Mexico. You don't know about it. Sam the Lion died yesterday mornin'."

"Died?" Sonny said. After a moment he walked over to the curb in front of the courthouse and sat down. The traffic light blinked red and green over the empty street. Andy came over to the curb too, yawning and rubbing the back of his neck.

"Yep," he said. "Quite a blow. Keeled over on one of the snooker tables. Had a stroke."

Soon it was dawn, a cool, dewy spring dawn that wet the courthouse grass and left a low white mist on the pastures for the sun to burn away. Andy sat on the fender of his Nash and told all about the death and how everybody had taken it, who had cried and who hadn't. "Good thing you all got back today, you'd 'a missed the funeral," he said. "How'd you find Mexico?" Sonny could not have told him; he had lost track of things and just wanted to sit on the curb and watch the traffic light change.

Questions for Critical Thinking and Writing

1. Why do you think Duane and Sonny decided to travel to Mexico? What did they expect to find there?

2. To what extent was it important for McMurtry to include the description of the three boys sleeping in the house that Duane and Sonny visit? Where else in this section does McMurtry write about Mexican children?

3. Ruth is mentioned on several occasions in this excerpt, but not described as a character. What, based on this excerpt, do you think she is like? What purpose does she serve in this passage?

4. How are Duane and Sonny alike? How are they different? Compare and contrast these characters in a brief essay, using examples from the text as evidence.

LARRY McMURTRY

For a biographical note on Larry McMurtry, see page 109.

BEFORE YOU READ

In the following commentary, Larry McMurtry writes that to be a Texas writer means to suffer an "amusing fate," to be "a regionalist from an unpopular region." Consider McMurtry's use of humor. Are Texas writers, as McMurtry notes, thought of as boring or even "dangerously vulgar"? Or is Texas a "literary capital"?

On Being a Texas Writer   1968

Being a writer and a Texan is an amusing fate, one that gets funnier as one's sense of humor darkens. In times like these it verges on the macabre. Apparently there was a time in the forties and fifties when people sort of enjoyed reading about Texas, if the reading was light enough. The state was thought to be different — another country, almost. . . .

Alas, all is changed. We aren't thought of as quaintly vulgar anymore. Some may find us *dangerously* vulgar, but the majority just find us boring. As a subject, Texas has become frankly stultifying: if it's another country, it's a country literate America hopes to hear no more about. . . .

As a regionalist, and a regionalist from an unpopular region, I find the problem of how to get heard rather a fascinating one. I haven't found it especially depressing, but then I wouldn't have gone in for writing if I hadn't liked talking to myself. I quite recognize that there have always been literary capitals and literary provinces, and that those who choose for whatever reason to abide in the provinces need not expect a modish recognition. Recently, of course, the picture has become much brighter. The Texas writer who really wants to get famous has only to work up his autobiography in such a way that it will (1) explain the assassination [of John F. Kennedy] and (2) make it possible for President Johnson to be impeached.° If he can do that, his name is made. *The New York Review of Books* will beat a path to his door, particularly if his door happens to be somewhere in Manhattan. Should his door be in Anarene, Texas, they will probably rely on the mails, but in any event he can put obscurity behind him. If he ever gets to New York he may even meet Susan Sontag.

I don't understand the assassination and I doubt that I can do anything about the President. My chances of meeting Miss Sontag are accordingly pretty slim and I might as well forget about it and go on and write a book about the place where my characters live.

QUESTIONS FOR CRITICAL THINKING AND WRITING

1. Do you think, as McMurtry asserts, that literary America now finds Texas "boring"? Why?

When McMurtry wrote this essay (1968), Lyndon B. Johnson (1908–1973) was the U.S. president. Johnson served from 1963 to 1969.

2. Why do you think New York City is the other region focused on in this commentary?

3. Based on your reading of McMurtry's story earlier in the anthology, do you think he follows his own advice on the best approach to writing? Do you think he'd be a lesser writer if he changed his subject matter?

4. **CONNECT TO ANOTHER READING.** In a short essay, compare McMurtry's comments with Don Graham's "Lone Star Literature" (p. 7). Where do their thoughts on the perception of Texas literature match up? Do they differ in any respects? How do you think each one feels about the influence of Texas on their own writing and the writing of others?

HARRYETTE MULLEN

Harryette Mullen was born in Florence, Alabama, in 1953. She grew up in Fort Worth, Texas, and graduated from the University of Texas, Austin. Of her childhood, Mullen once said, "Although in my family of preachers and teachers a girl was expected to grow up a lady, I was fascinated by those black women in the community who had no interest in ladylikeness." She is the author of seven published poetry collections, including *Blues Baby: Early Poems*, in which the following two poems were first published, *Muse & Drudge*, and, most recently, *Recyclopedia*. Throughout her writing and teaching careers, Mullen has earned such honors as a Rockefeller Fellowship, a grant from the Foundation for Contemporary Arts, and a fellowship from the John Simon Guggenheim Memorial Foundation. She is currently associate professor of English and African American studies at the University of California, Los Angeles.

BEFORE YOU READ

In the following poems, Harryette Mullen explores relationships with girlfriends, mothers, and daughters. In "Las Locas," what is the narrator's connection to the "crazy girls from Laredo"? What everyday details does the poet weave in to bring the "locas" to life? As you read the second poem, "Momma Sayings," pay attention to the poet's use of language and quotations. How do these work to create a voice for the other? What is that mother like? What are her attitudes toward her children?

Las Locas   *1981*
for Angélica y Cristina

Oh, you crazy girls from Laredo
I'll always remember you

heating tortillas on an ironingboard
in the freshman dorm

dyeing your straight shiny black hair   5
even blacker and shinier
telephone black
mystery black of ladies
with unlisted numbers

going to dances in gold and silver *puta* shoes   10

and getting me so drunk on tequila
I slid down the stairs
at a party fundraiser

You crazy giggling girls
calling yourselves *Chichas y Chones*   15

From you I learned to eat refried beans
for breakfast,
beans you cooked with beer and cilantro
instead of fatback

You gave me *la llorona* and the evil eye   20
and *abrazoed* me into your *raza*

You girls, you *locas*
spoke Spanish to me whether I could *comprende* or not
and if I didn't know all the words
        I understood your voices   25

Momma Sayings   *1981*

Momma had words for us:
We were "crumb crushers,"
"eating machines,"
"bottomless pits."
Still, she made us charter members   5
of the bonepickers' club,
saying, "Just don't let your eyes
get bigger than your stomachs."
Saying, "Take all you want,
but eat all you take."   10
Saying, "I'm not made of money, you know,
and the man at the Safeway
don't give away groceries for free."

She trained us not to leave lights on
"all over the house,"   15
because "electricity costs money —
so please turn the light off when you leave a room
and take the white man's hand out of my pocket."

When we were small
she called our feet "ant mashers,"   20

but when we'd outgrow our shoes,
our feet became "platforms."
She told us we must be growing big feet
to support some big heavyset women
(like our grandma Tiddly).   25

When she had to buy us new underwear
to replace the old ones full of holes,
she'd swear we were growing razor blades in our behinds,
"you tear these drawers up so fast."

Momma had words for us, alright: 30
She called us "the wrecking crew."
She said our bedroom
looked like "a cyclone struck it."

Our dirty fingernails she called "victory gardens."
And when we'd come in from playing outside   35
she'd tell us, "You smell like iron rust."
She'd say, "Go take a bath
and get some of that funk off you."
But when the water ran too long in the tub
she'd yell, "That's enough water to wash an elephant."   40
And after the bath she'd say,
"Be sure and grease those ashy legs."
She'd lemon-cream our elbows
and pull the hot comb
through "these tough kinks on your heads."   45

Momma had lots of words for us,
her never quite perfect daughters,
the two brown pennies
she wanted to polish
so we'd shine like dimes.   50

QUESTIONS FOR CRITICAL THINKING AND WRITING

1. What details about the girls described in "Las Locas" are most memorable to you? Why? Explain your answer by quoting from the text.

2. In "Las Locas," what is the author's purpose in using Spanish words and phrases without providing English translations? How does this choice relate to the final stanza of the poem? That is, to what extent can you understand the voice of the poem itself, without understanding all of its words?

3. What does the speaker in the poem "Las Locas" mean when she says: "You . . . *abrazoed* me into your *raza*"? How do las locas "adopt" the poem's speaker?

4. In "Momma Sayings," how do concerns about money—as well as appearance and social respectability—shape the mother's attitudes?

5. Reread "Momma Sayings," with an eye and ear toward language. Which of the mother's sayings are particularly vivid? How do these word choices contribute to the poem's overall effect? To its humor? Is the mother a likeable character? Why or why not? And, finally, how do the mother's "sayings" throughout the first six stanzas compare with the tone of the final stanza? What, if anything, is resolved there?

6. **CONNECT TO ANOTHER READING.** Compare Mullen's use of everyday details in her poems with the observations that Naomi Shihab Nye (p. 130) makes in her poems. In what ways do these poets set a magnifying glass on the ordinary? And to what effect(s)?

MYTHS FROM NATIVE AMERICAN TRIBES OF TEXAS: CADDO, KIOWA-APACHE, AND TEJAS/HASINAI

Their oral culture suggests the Caddo people were originally from the Arkansas region and dispersed to the South and West. The Caddo encounters with Europeans began with Hernando de Soto and his men in Texas in 1542. Caddo tribes were moved from Texas in 1859 and settled by the government on a reservation in Oklahoma.

The Kiowa-Apache, also called the Plains Apache, lived primarily in and around the Texas panhandle. They were one of the six subtribes of the Apache people. In 1905, there were only 155 members of the Kiowa-Apache left. Most of the remaining members of the tribe currently live in Oklahoma, and their spoken language is nearly extinct.

The Tejas or Hasinai tribes are linked to the Caddo by a common language. Spanish explorers encountered these peoples in East Texas and named them "Tejas," based on the Caddo word for "friend" (which later also became "Texas").

BEFORE YOU READ

Caddo, Kiowa-Apache, and Tejas (or Hasinai) are the names of a few of the Native American tribes that once populated the southwestern region of the United States. How do the legends of the indigenous peoples of Texas shed light on their beliefs about themselves and about the world in which they lived? What do the following myths have in common with legends and fairy tales from other cultures?

Caddo Tribe *Coyote and the Seven Brothers*

Long ago, an old woman lived with her seven sons in a lodge at the edge of the woods. All of her sons were fine hunters, and every evening they brought home more game than the eight of them could eat. The old woman was kept busy from sunrise to sunset cooking their meals and drying the meat they could not eat.

One day the old woman's eldest son went hunting and did not come home. After three days his dogs returned, but he did not.

The next day the old woman's second son said, "Do not worry, Mother. I will go and find my brother." And he took the dogs and set out. After three days the dogs came back, but neither he nor his brother were with them.

The third brother said, "Do not worry, Mother. I will go and find my brothers."

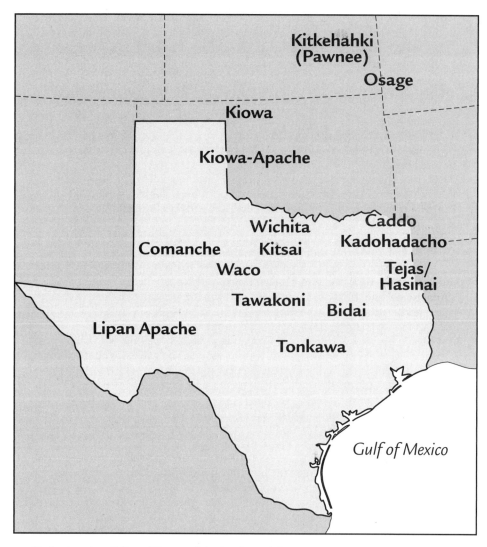

Native American Tribes of Texas and the Southern Plains.

But, again, the dogs returned alone.

The fourth, fifth, and sixth brothers, each in turn, went out to search for his lost brothers, but each time the dogs came home days later alone.

"Mother," said Small Brother, the seventh son. "I must go and find my brothers."

But his mother was frightened. "No, no!" she cried. "You cannot! If you go, I will lose you, too. You will never return. You must not go."

Small Brother was sad, but he stayed at home. One day when his brothers had been gone for a long time, he was playing in front of the lodge when he saw a raccoon sitting in a tree at the edge of the woods.

"Mother, Mother!" he called. "A raccoon is sitting in a tree at the edge of the woods. If you will bring me my bow and arrows, we will have fresh meat tonight."

"I will," answered the old woman, and she brought out his bow and arrows.

Small Brother called the dogs. The raccoon saw the boy and the dogs coming, and jumped to the next tree, and the next and the next. Small Brother followed it deep into the woods, until at last it ran up a tree and down a big hole in its trunk. The boy climbed up and reached down into the tree to grasp the raccoon by the tail.

"Hoh, boy!" a strange voice called.

Small Brother looked down and saw a little old woman with a sharp, pointed nose.

"Drop the raccoon down here," the old woman said. "Your dogs and I will kill it." So Small Brother threw the raccoon down. The old woman killed it, but when he was not looking, she killed one of his dogs, too. "Look in the tree," she called. "There is another raccoon."

Small Brother looked, and there was, so he threw that one down to her. She killed that one too, and when he was not looking, she killed another dog.

"I see *another* raccoon," Small Brother called happily, and he reached down and pulled that one out, and threw it down to the old woman. Four . . . five . . . six raccoons he threw down, and the old woman killed them, and with each one, another dog. Small Brother was about to pull the seventh and last raccoon out from the hole in the tree when suddenly it spoke to him.

"Little boy," it said, "that old woman is a witch. It was she who killed your brothers. Now she has killed all of your dogs, and she will kill you next if you do not run. You must pull me out and throw me as far from the tree as you can. I will run off, and the old witch will chase me. Then you must run home as fast as your feet can fly."

Small Brother looked down and saw that it was so. All of his dogs were gone. "I will," he said. He threw the seventh raccoon as far as he could, jumped down from the tree, and ran away home.

The witch returned to the tree when she had found the last raccoon and killed it, and was angry to find the little boy gone. She chased after him, but he was so far ahead that she could not catch him.

The boy told his mother all that had happened. That night he had a strange dream. In the morning he told the dream to his mother. "In the dream," he said, "I was walking along, and I met Coyote. He told me that my brothers are not dead. A wicked chief and his people captured them and made them slaves. They must work so hard that they will die if they do not get away. And, Mother, Coyote promised to help!"

"Then he will," said his old mother.

That afternoon Small Brother went out hunting. Just as in his dream, he met Coyote as he was walking along. Just as in his dream, Coyote told him that his brothers were not dead.

"A wicked chief and his people have captured them and made them their slaves," Coyote said. "They must work so hard that they will die if they do not get away, so I am on my way to help them."

Small Brother went home to tell his mother, and Coyote went on through the woods. Soon he spied Flying Squirrel. Flying Squirrel was hard at work filling a big basket with pecan nuts.

"Give me some pecans, friend," Coyote said. "You have too big a load to fly with."

"Then I must drag it," Flying Squirrel answered. He gave a nervous look over his shoulder. "The pecans are for Wicked Chief, who is my master. I cannot give you even one."

Coyote was pleased. "Hoh! You're just the fellow I was looking for. What is your master like? And does he still have six brothers for servants, and are they well?"

Flying Squirrel chattered away at great speed. He told Coyote that Wicked Chief was a monster with a long, pointed beak of a nose, that he lived across the wide river, that his people were almost as bad as he, and that the six brothers were still alive, but if the bad people killed them, they would eat them.

"Hoh! Well, I am here to help those brothers get away. Your monster chief cannot be as clever as I, and I have great magic," Coyote bragged. "All I need is a way to cross the wide river."

"If you hold on to my tail as I fly, I will take you across," Flying Squirrel offered.

"I can do that," Coyote said. So, off they went, soaring over the river, but Flying Squirrel's tail was so silky smooth that Coyote's paws began to slip. He slip-slip-slipped right off the end of it just before they reached the far bank of the river, and he fell into the water. He crawled out and hid in the tall grass to shake himself dry, and to think. "Hah!" he said to himself at last. "I will turn myself into a new corn grinder!"

So he did. The new hollowed-out stone grinding mill and its grinder stone slithered into the river and floated down to Wicked Chief's camp. Before long one of the women of the bad people came down to the riverbank with her water jar, and saw the mill.

"Hoh! I could use that," she said. When she could not reach it, she ran back to ask Wicked Chief to get it for her.

"A stone corn mill that floats?" the monster snorted. "Someone is playing a trick. It must be Coyote."

"I say it is a corn mill, and a fine one," the woman shouted. "And I want it."

The chief grumbled, but he sent someone to fish the corn mill out of the river. All of the bad women liked it so much that they took turns pounding their corn in it. "It is the best mill we have ever had," they said.

But the next day, the first bad woman was grinding fine sweet corn and looked down to see that all of her corn was gone. She dropped the grinder and ran to tell the chief.

"I told you that mill was Coyote," Wicked Chief growled. "Bring it to me."

When the woman brought it, he set it on the big log where he skewered prisoners with his long, spiked nose. "Take that, Coyote!" the monster crowed as he raised up his head and speared down with his nose. But as he did, the corn mill rolled off the log and turned into Coyote. Wicked Chief's nose was stuck so deep into the log that it never came out, and he could never move.

Coyote called together all of the slaves and told them they were free. Then he sent the six brothers home to their mother and Small Brother. Always afterward, when the seven brothers killed any game for their dinner, they left a share of the meat behind for Coyote.

Kiowa-Apache Tribe   *Coyote Makes the Sun*

In the very first days of the First Days, the earth and the sky were dark. Coyote°
had heard that many animal people lived nearby in the darkness, and he went
looking for them. One by one, he found Black Hawk and Jackrabbit, Prairie
Chicken and Turtle.

To each he said, "You are just the one I need. You must come to a council
tonight to see what we can do about this darkness and the cold."

At the council that night, Black Hawk, Jackrabbit, Prairie Chicken, and
Turtle sat in a circle and shivered while Coyote explained why he had brought
them together. "This cold and this darkness have lasted long enough," he
began.

"Hoh, yes!" squawked Prairie Chicken. "And we are just the ones to put an
end to it."

"Hai! We are!" shrieked Black Hawk.

"Yes, we are!" Coyote echoed. "So we must try to make daylight."

Turtle frowned. "How?" he asked.

But Jackrabbit leaped up in excitement. "Yes, yes, *yes!*"

"And perhaps we can get fire for all of the animal people," Coyote went on.

"Where?" Turtle asked.

Coyote grinned. "I know the place. Not long ago, I passed a cave in a high
bank. When the little people there opened the door, some light spilled out.
They were the Bug People, and inside their cave I saw fire. It made the cave as
bright as day, but then the people shut the door again. They only open it up for
their own people to come in. Their fire is only for themselves."

Black Hawk, Jackrabbit, Prairie Chicken, and Turtle scowled and muttered
when they heard that.

"Now," said Coyote, "how are we going to get it?"

Black Hawk and Prairie Chicken piped up together. "We can see you have a
plan," they said. "Tell us."

Coyote puffed out his chest a little. "It is this," he said. "I will go along to
that cave to spy out how they guard their fire. I want to see who guards the
door. You must follow behind, and wait where I tell you."

So the five of them set out.

When they had gone a little way, Coyote said to Turtle, "Wait here," and
went on with the others. "Wait here," Coyote said to Prairie Chicken after a
while. Jackrabbit was left behind next, and Black Hawk last. Coyote went on
alone.

When he came near the place where he thought the cave was, he sat down
to watch and wait. After a while he saw a crack of light as a door began to open.
The door in the hill swung out, and in the light that spilled through it, he saw
one of the little bug people. It was Dragonfly. "What luck!" thought Coyote.
Dragonfly could not turn his head, so he could look only straight ahead. All
Coyote had to do was to creep up behind him to catch him.

So he did.

"*Skree-eek!*" squeaked Dragonfly. His wings fluttered in fright.

Coyote is a trickster figure common to many Native American myths. Coyote, sometimes
clever and funny, other times greedy or reckless, is usually a male character who can change
shapes.

Coyote growled softly. "Hoh, you! What are you doing out here?"

"Watching!" Dragonfly squeaked. "Only watching. I watch the door to be sure that only Bug People go in. I can see only straight ahead, so the people know I am a good watcher. My eyes never wander. If I say 'Open the door,' they open it."

Coyote grinned. "Good. And I have you now, little bug! Shall I squash you or let you go? If you will call out to the people to open the door, I will set you free."

"Then they will kill me!" Dragonfly squeaked.

Coyote shrugged. "You can fly away. They cannot see you in the dark." He gave Dragonfly a little pinch.

"Aow!" Dragonfly shrieked, and quickly called out, "You people inside! Open the door!" Then, as soon as Coyote let him go, he skittered away into the darkness.

The door opened. Inside Coyote saw a large, bright room, a bright fire set in a circle of stones, and all of the Bug People dancing. They laughed and hopped and twirled. Everyone else on the earth was miserable, but the Bug People were happy and dancing. Coyote stepped in.

The people stopped dancing. "Hoh, Big One!" they cried. "How did you get in? Who let you in?"

"I let myself in," Coyote said. "Oh, please, good people, let me stay! I love dancing. I will work for you — I will carry the food to your cooks by the fire — if only I can join in your dance."

The Bug People were still feeling happy from the dancing, so they squeaked, "Very well. Come in and shut the door and dance."

The people laughed when they saw Coyote's wild dancing. He skipped and bobbed and whirled, coming closer to the fire with each twirl.

"Look out!" the Bug People called. "Your tail will catch fire! Your tail will catch fire!"

Coyote laughed and whirled again. "I don't care! I love to dance!"

He danced and danced, and then, when he was close enough to the fire, he put his tail right into it, scooped up coals and flame with it, and dashed for the door. The Bug People chased after him. They shouted to one another, "Stop him! Stop him! Stop him!"

Coyote ran so fast that it was not long before he grew tired. He was almost at the place where Black Hawk was waiting, so he called out, "Hawk! Hawk!"

Black Hawk swooped down, took up the coals on his own tail, and flew off with the Bug People whizzing behind. He drew as far ahead as he could, and when he came to the place where Jackrabbit waited, he passed the fire to him. Jackrabbit ran until he, too, was tired. Then Prairie Chicken took the fire from him, and flew with it to meet Turtle. The Bug People were so close behind by then that Turtle only had time to shut himself inside his shell with the coals.

"Open up! Open up!" cried the Bug People. They knocked on Turtle's shell. They shouted at the place where only the beak over his mouth showed. They rocked his shell back and forth. Nothing would make him come out.

"Roll him down into the river!" called some. So they did. Turtle rolled over and over, plopped into the water, and sank. The Bug People waited for a while, but at last they gave up and went home.

Coyote and Black Hawk, Jackrabbit and Prairie Chicken had come up just as Turtle rolled into the water. They hid in the tall grass until the Bug People were gone, then ran to help Turtle out of the stream. Then they gathered some wood and made a big fire with the coals Turtle had saved.

"Now," Coyote asked, "what shall we do with fire?" And he answered himself, "*I* think we should make daylight."

His companions agreed, for that was why they had come in the first place. "You know how. You make it," they said. So Coyote took the fire and rolled it into a sun, and suddenly everything around was bright with daylight.

Coyote was pleased with himself. "Good! Now, where will we put it?"

Before Coyote could answer his own question again, Black Hawk and Prairie Chicken flew up to the top of the highest mountain. "Up here! Let us put it up here," they called.

"No," Coyote shouted back. "The people who live too far away to see the mountain will not be able to see it there." He turned to the sun. "Sun, I am going to throw you up into the sky. Up there you can roll around and give daylight to everyone."

Coyote did just that. Coyote's companions cheered as Sun shone out across the world, but Coyote was not finished. Some fire still was left.

"What shall we do with this last bit?" Coyote asked. The others waited for him to answer himself, and he did. "I say we should put fire into rocks, and give rocks to everyone."

So he did, and today fire rocks still hold fire. People still can strike two fire rocks together, and with tinder and dry wood make a fire for cooking and keeping warm. And the Bug People cannot steal it back.

Kiowa-Apache Tribe   *How Poor Boy Won His Wife*

Poor Boy had no family. None of the Apaches of his tribe cared for him, though some gave him food. He had no weapon, so hunting was hard. Sometimes he fished in the creek. Sometimes he went out at night to set snares for jackrabbits. One night, out on a hill not far from the camp, he heard the sound of weeping.

He crept around to the shadow side of the hill, and upward. On top of the hill, a girl sat in the moonlight, weeping for her brother, who had been killed far away, in a fight with Comanches.

"Ai, ai!" the girl mourned. "I miss him so! Our parents cannot even say a blessing over his bones. If I could only see his bones! If only some brave were to bring me one of his bones, even the smallest of his little-finger bones, I would . . . I would marry him!"

"What did you say?" asked a voice.

The girl turned and saw Poor Boy standing not far away. She spoke through her tears. "I said that if any brave brings me even one of my brother's bones, I will marry him."

"Then I am going to find your brother's bones and bring them home," Poor Boy said quietly. "Come stand on this spot on this hill each day and watch to the northeast, toward the Comanche country. Keep watch, for I will return."

Then Poor Boy went down the hill to a place where he could be alone, and pray. At dawn, in his mind, his spirit spoke to him. "Do you see that great dust in the distance?" it said. "It is from the hooves of the horses of the Comanche. There is where you will find her brother."

So Poor Boy journeyed to the Comanche country. When he came there, the Comanches were holding a Sun Dance. All day, Poor Boy sat behind a tree on a hill a long way off, and watched. As he watched, his spirit spoke to him again. "You will find Brother at the center of the lodge at the center of the camp," it said. But too many people were there. Many were dancing. Many more watched the dancing. "I will wait until night, and creep close then," thought Poor Boy.

After dark, he crept down to the open-sided lodge that was the dancing shelter. Some people were still there, so he sat in the shadows and listened. As he listened, he seemed to hear a long sigh overhead, and a voice that whispered, *"Hoh, I am tired, so tired."* Poor Boy looked up at the fork of the center pole. He saw a young man tied there hand and foot. It was the girl's brother, and he was alive!

Poor Boy sat looking up and trying to think of a plan. Even if he could climb so high, he would be seen, and caught.

"If only," he wished, "someone here had a kind heart and would help me help him!"

"Very well," a tiny voice answered. "*I* will help."

Poor Boy looked down and saw a spider sitting beside him.

"I will help," the spider said. "Climb this pole, and I will follow."

Poor Boy was about to say, "I cannot — they will see me," when he looked down and saw that he himself had become a spider. At once he raced up the nearest pole as fast as his eight legs would take him. From the top, he ran along a crossbeam to the center pole. Spider followed close behind.

"I am so tired," the girl's brother whispered. "I am so tired."

"All is well, Brother-in-Law," Poor Boy piped up in his small spider's voice. "I have come to take you home."

Poor Boy and Spider cut through the cords that bound the young man. To his surprise, when he tried to rub his wrists, he found that he, too, had become a spider. Together, the three spiders raced along the wooden beam to the pole at the outer rim. Before they climbed down, Spider warned the other two that great dangers awaited them.

"The Comanches will chase you, for as soon as your feet touch ground, you will be human beings, not spiders. They will see you, but before they capture you, you must run into the tipi of their chief. The chief and his wife are alone there. His people will gather around the tipi, but they will not enter. The chief will test you, and if you pass his tests, you will have a chance to escape. When you go, the Comanche people will chase you, but they cannot kill you unless you look back. You may stop four times to catch your breath, but do not look back. No matter what you hear behind you, do not look back!"

The two Apache boys did as Spider told them. When they reached the foot of the pole and saw that they had their own hands and feet and selves back, they ran straight to the chief's tipi. The Comanche people shouted and ran after them, but stopped in the doorway. No one followed Poor Boy and the girl's brother inside.

The Comanche chief looked at the two young men. When at last he spoke, he said, "You both are brave, but my people wish to kill you. We will smoke a pipe together, and I will decide what to do." He held out two pipes, one black and one red. "Choose which you will smoke."

Spider had told them, "Be sure to take the black pipe. If you take the red one, they can kill you." So the two young men chose the black, and the people at the doorway muttered angrily.

After the chief had filled and lit the black pipe, each young man took a puff, and then Poor Boy handed it back to the chief. The chief put it aside and offered them next two drinking bowls. One held red water. One held black water. The boys remembered Spider's second warning. "Be sure to take the black drink," he had told them. "If you take the red one, they will kill you." So they took the black water and, between them, drank it down.

"I have decided," the chief said. "You may go." He gave a wave of his hand, and the Comanche people moved back to let them pass.

The young men ran.

As soon as they passed out of the Comanche camp and over the brow of the hill beyond, the people started running after them. They shouted as they ran. The chase went on and on into the night. When the boys had to stop to catch their breath, they could hear the yells of the Comanches as they drew closer. The boys were frightened, but they did not look back. They caught their breath and set off again running. After another hour they had to stop again. This time, the cries of the Comanches sounded close at their backs. The boys trembled, but did not look behind them. They caught their breath, then ran again.

When they stopped to rest the third time, the shouts of the Comanches were so close in their ears that it seemed they would run right over them. The boys jumped up in alarm, but even in their fright they remembered Spider's words, and did not look back as they ran on. When they stopped for the fourth time to rest, they heard nothing but silence.

The remainder of their journey went swiftly. Near dawn they saw that they had come almost to their own camp. In the camp, the girl rose just before daylight and went up onto the hill as she did every morning. When she looked out across the land, she saw the figures of two men coming across the prairie.

"Brother! Oh, my brother!" she shouted as she ran to meet him. She threw her arms about her brother, then led him back to the camp. As they went, she called out to everyone, "It is my brother! My brother is home again!"

"My son, we thought you were dead," cried his father. "How have you come back to us? Who brought you home?"

"This fellow," his son said. He pulled his companion forward.

"Poor Boy? He has brought you?" The old man was surprised, but then he heard of the girl's promise. He saw the cuts on his son's wrists and ankles from the cords. He listened to the boys' tale. "Wife," he said, "prepare a feast for our daughter's husband." And she did. And to every guest who came, the old man told the tale, and he pointed out Poor Boy and proudly called him Son-in-Law.

And that is how Poor Boy won the wife he wanted.

Tejas/Hasinai Tribe   *The Beginning of the World*

Ayo-Caddi-Aymay, as the Tejas people called God, was the one and only God, and whatever he did turned out for the best. But, said the Tejas, he had help. At the beginning of the First Time, when there was only earth and darkness, Old Man appeared. In his hand he held an acorn, and the acorn opened and grew—

not into an oak tree, but into a magical woman. Old Man wished to make a heaven, and so together he and Acorn Woman put in place a great circle of timber to hold up the sky. The timber circle was so wide that if you looked off toward the west, the dry mountains hid it. To the north, the grass of the rolling prairie hid it. To the south, the far edge of the sea hid it, and to the east it was hidden by the green hills. When the work was finished, Acorn Woman climbed up into the heavens, where every day she still gives new birth to the sun and moon, to rain, frost, and snow, to lightning and thunder, and to the corn.

In the world under the new sky there lived only one woman, and in time she had two daughters. One day when the sisters were out by themselves gathering food, a huge and terrible monster charged out of the bushes, straight at them. *"Caddaja!"* the girls cried as they turned and ran. "A devil! A demon!" Its red eyes blazed like hot coals, and its horns were so wide that their tips stretched out of sight.

One girl was not quick enough. The *caddaja* snatched at her, caught her in its claws, gobbled her up, swallowed her down, and looked around for her sister. Her sister had run on until she came to a very tall pine tree. Its faraway top seemed the safest place to hide. She climbed up to the very tip of the topmost branch, but the giant *caddaja* sniffed out her path. It lifted up its ugly head and spied the shadow of her shape through the pine boughs.

It tried to climb the tree, but fell back. It tried again and fell back again, for it was too heavy for climbing.

It tried with its sharp claws and strong horns to cut down the tree or break it. The tree was strong, but it groaned and whipped back and forth. The girl knew as she clung fast to her branch that the tree could not hold out for long. She looked down.

Below, on one side of the tree, the monster rammed the tree trunk and roared. At the foot of the tree on the other side lay a small pond. The girl knew its waters, black and deep. Quickly she unwrapped her legs from the branch, dangled for a moment, held her breath, and dropped straight down. Down, down through the water she went, like an arrow. The angry *caddaja* ran around the tree and bent to suck up the water. As he sucked, he spewed it away so that he could scoop her up from the bottom. But he did not find her.

She had fooled him. Below ground, a hidden stream fed the pond, and the girl swam along it. She came up far away, where the stream flowed out into the sunshine, and ran home to tell her mother all that had happened. Afterward, she and her mother returned to the place where the sister had died. There, caught in an acorn cup, they found a single drop of blood. They covered it with another acorn cup, and the mother placed it safely in her bosom for the journey home. Once there, she put it in a pottery jar, covered the mouth of the jar, and set it in a corner.

In the night, the mother heard a scratching sound that seemed to come from the jar. She went to look. When she uncovered the jar, she discovered that the drop of blood had grown into a little boy no bigger than her little finger. Startled, she replaced the cover on the jar. The next night she and her daughter heard the same noise. When they sat up in alarm, they saw the jar break, and a full-grown young man step out.

"Grandson!" the mother cried out in joy, and embraced him. "Oh, welcome, son of my daughter!"

The young man looked around. "Where is my mother?"

His grandmother and aunt told him of the terrible *caddaja*, of his mother's death, and of the blood drop in the acorn cup.

"I will find it! I will find that giant demon and kill it!" the Blood-Drop Boy cried out.

So his grandmother made him a bow and an arrow, and the next morning he set out. When at last he found the giant monster, he raised his bow and shot his arrow so deep into it that the monster fled, and was never seen again.

Yet that *caddaja* was only one of the many that hated all human beings and caused great terror among the first people. When Blood-Drop Boy returned home, his grandmother and aunt told him that a world full of *caddajas* was so frightening that they wished to leave it. The rest of the men and women and children who had appeared on earth after Grandmother were turning themselves into animal people—bears, otters, dogs, deer, coyotes—to escape the hatred of the monsters.

"It is not yet a good world for humans," Grandmother said. "Perhaps one day it will be. But for us, let us go up to *Cachao-ayo*, the sky above, and watch over the earth from there."

So Blood-Drop Boy went up into the heavens with them, and for all the days and years that followed watched over and guided the world below.

QUESTIONS FOR CRITICAL THINKING AND WRITING

1. What similar themes do these legends from different Native American tribes share?

2. Who is Coyote? Is he the same character in both the Caddo and the Kiowa-Apache myths? Explain.

3. What role do humans play in these myths? What are their relationships to each other? To animal characters?

4. For some of the tribes represented by these stories, these legends offer the only clues left about past traditions and beliefs. Choose one of these tales and explain in a short essay why you think it was told. What does it teach about the world the tribe lived in? What does it preserve of the tribe's culture?

NAOMI SHIHAB NYE

Naomi Shihab Nye was born in St. Louis, Missouri, in 1952 to a Palestinian father and an American mother. She spent parts of her youth in Jordan and Jerusalem, and also in San Antonio, Texas, where she currently resides. Nye's published works of poetry include *Different Ways to Pray, You and Yours, 19 Varieties of Gazelle: Poems of the Middle East, Fuel, Red Suitcase,* and *Hugging the Jukebox.* Nye has also collected Texan art and writing in an anthology called *Is This Forever, or What: Poems & Paintings from Texas.* A novelist and songwriter, in addition to being a poet, she holds awards from the Texas Institute of Letters and the International Poetry Forum and has won four Pushcart Prizes. Fellow poet William Stafford has said of Nye: "She is a champion of the literature of encouragement and heart." The following two poems are from *Words Under the Words: Selected Poems.*

BEFORE YOU READ

In her poem "Hello," Nye reveals the details of a usually hidden natural world and identifies moments of birth and realization. Are these moments tender? Appalling? Some combination? She addresses the seemingly ordinary again in "Famous." What is the importance of the relationships she describes? Who does the narrator of "Famous" want to be — and why?

Hello *1995*

Some nights
the rat with pointed teeth
makes his long way back
to the bowl of peaches.
He stands on the dining room table 5
sinking his tooth
drinking the pulp
of each fruity turned-up face
knowing you will read
this message and scream. 10
It is his only text,
to take and take in darkness,
to be gone before you awaken
and your giant feet
start creaking the floor. 15

Where is the mother of the rat?
The father, the shredded nest,
which breath were we taking
when the rat was born,
when he lifted his shivering snout 20
to rafter and rivet and stone?
I gave him the names of the devil,
seared and screeching names,
I would not enter those rooms
without a stick to guide me, 25
I leaned on the light, shuddering,
and the moist earth under the house,
the trailing tails of clouds,
said he was in the closet,
the drawer of candles, 30
his nose was a wick.

How would we live together
with our sad shoes and hideouts,
our lock on the door
and his delicate fingered paws   35
that could clutch and grip,
his blank slate of fur
and the pillow where we press our faces?
The bed that was a boat is sinking.
And the shores of morning loom up   40
lined with little shadows,
things we never wanted to be, or meet,
and all the rats are waving hello.

Famous   *1995*

The river is famous to the fish.

The loud voice is famous to silence,
which knew it would inherit the earth
before anybody said so.

The cat sleeping on the fence is famous to the birds   5
watching him from the birdhouse.

The tear is famous, briefly, to the cheek.

The idea you carry close to your bosom
is famous to your bosom.

The boot is famous to the earth,   10
more famous than the dress shoe,
which is famous only to floors.

The bent photograph is famous to the one who carries it
and not at all famous to the one who is pictured.

I want to be famous to shuffling men   15
who smile while crossing streets,
sticky children in grocery lines,
famous as the one who smiled back.

I want to be famous in the way a pulley is famous,
or a buttonhole, not because it did anything spectacular,   20
but because it never forgot what it could do.

Questions for Critical Thinking and Writing

1. Nye uses several pronouns (I, you, we) in the poem "Hello." Who do you
   think the pronouns refer to? Explain using specific examples from the text.
2. What is the difference between the way the narrator of "Famous" hopes to
   be famous, and the ways to be famous described in the first seven stanzas?

3. If you were given these two poems without the author's name attached to them, would you know that they are both by the same author? Draw from the poems to support your answer.

4. Explore the language and imagery in one or both of Nye's poems. What effect do they have on you as a reader? Is one poem more vivid and memorable than the other? If so, explain why, drawing on specific words and passages from the poem(s).

AMÉRICO PAREDES

Américo Paredes (1915–1999) was born in Brownsville, Texas. A Mexican American journalist, scholar, poet, and teacher, Paredes had great interest in the border region between Mexico and the United States. Paredes won many prizes and fellowships for his work as a writer, including a prize from the National Endowment for the Humanities and a Guggenheim Fellowship. He attended the University of Texas at Austin for his bachelor of arts degree, earned his master's and doctoral degrees there, and then taught at the university for most of his career. With His Pistol in His Hand: A Border Ballad and Its Hero, from which the following reading is drawn, was his published dissertation. In With His Pistol in His Hand, Paredes tells the story of Gregorio Cortez, a Texas-Mexican ranchhand who became legend following his 1901 pistol duel with a Texas sheriff. Throughout the narrative, Paredes threads the history and folklore of the Rio Grande region and Border Country along with his own interpretations. The following section is taken from part 1, "Gregorio Cortez, the Legend and the Life," chapter 1, "The Country."

BEFORE YOU READ

Have you ever heard the expression "shoot first, ask questions later"? In the following reading, Paredes discusses this course of action that was sometimes taken by the law-enforcement agency, the Texas Rangers. According to Paredes, how did the policies of the Rangers affect those living under their jurisdiction?

From *With His Pistol in His Hand:* The Texas Rangers

1958

The group of men who were most responsible for putting the Texan's pseudo folklore into deeds were the Texas Rangers. They were part of the legend themselves, its apotheosis as it were. If all the books written about the Rangers were put one on top of the other, the resulting pile would be almost as tall as some of the tales that they contain. The Rangers have been pictured as a fearless,

The Texas Rangers. The Texas Rangers were originally hired by Stephen F. Austin in 1823 to patrol the borders of the colony of Texas against Mexicans and the nearby Plains Indians. These men were poorly paid and had to provide their own weaponry. Shown here are Texas Rangers patrolling a river border in 1915.
© Bettmann/Corbis.

almost superhuman breed of men, capable of incredible feats. It may take a company of militia to quell a riot, but one Ranger was said to be enough for one mob. Evildoers, especially Mexican ones, were said to quail at the mere mention of the name. To the Ranger is given the credit for ending lawlessness and disorder along the Rio Grande.

The Ranger did make a name for himself along the Border. The word *rinche*, from "ranger," is an important one in Border folklore. It has been extended to cover not only the Rangers but any other Americans armed and mounted and looking for Mexicans to kill. Possemen and border patrolmen are also *rinches*, and even Pershing's cavalry is so called in Lower Border variants of ballads about the pursuit of Villa. The official Texas Rangers are known as the *rinches de la Kineña* or Rangers of King Ranch, in accordance with the Borderer's belief that the Rangers were the personal strong-arm men of Richard King and the other "cattle barons."

What the Border Mexican thought about the Ranger is best illustrated by means of sayings and anecdotes. Here are a few that are typical.

1. The Texas Ranger always carries a rusty old gun in his saddlebags. This is for use when he kills an unarmed Mexican. He drops the gun beside the body and then claims he killed the Mexican in self-defense and after a furious battle.

2. When he has to kill an armed Mexican, the Ranger tries to catch him asleep, or he shoots the Mexican in the back.

3. If it weren't for the American soldiers, the Rangers wouldn't dare come to the Border. The Ranger always runs and hides behind the soldiers when real trouble starts.

4. Once an army detachment was chasing a raider, and they were led by a couple of Rangers. The Mexican went into the brush. The Rangers galloped up to the place, pointed it out, and then stepped back to let the soldiers go in first.

5. Two Rangers are out looking for a Mexican horse thief. They strike his trail, follow it for a while, and then turn at right angles and ride until they meet a half-dozen Mexican laborers walking home from the fields. These they shoot with their deadly Colts. Then they go to the nearest town and send back a report to Austin: "In pursuit of horse thieves we encountered a band of Mexicans, and though outnumbered we succeeded in killing a dozen of them after a hard fight, without loss to ourselves. It is believed that others of the band escaped and are making for the Rio Grande." And as one can see, except for a few omissions and some slight exaggeration, the report is true in its basic details. Austin is satisfied that all is well on the Border. The Rangers add to their reputation as a fearless, hard-fighting breed of men; and the real horse thief stays out of the surrounding territory for some time, for fear he may meet up with the Rangers suddenly on some lonely road one day, and they may mistake him for a laborer.

I do not claim for these little tidbits the documented authenticity that Ranger historians claim for their stories. What we have here is frankly partisan and exaggerated without a doubt, but it does throw some light on Mexican attitudes toward the Ranger which many Texans may scarcely suspect. And it may be that these attitudes are not without some basis in fact.

The Rangers have been known to exaggerate not only the numbers of Mexicans they engaged but those they actually killed and whose bodies could be produced, presumably. In 1859 Cortina was defeated by a combined force of American soldiers and Texas Rangers. Army Major Heintzelman placed Cortina's losses at sixty; Ranger Captain Ford estimated them at two hundred.[1] In 1875 Ranger Captain McNelly climaxed his Red Raid on the Rio Grande by wiping out a band of alleged cattle rustlers at Palo Alto. McNelly reported fifteen dead; eight bodies were brought into Brownsville.[2] One more instance should suffice. In 1915 a band of about forty *sediciosos* (seditionists) under Aniceto Pizaña raided Norias in King Ranch. Three days later they were said to have been surrounded a mile from the Rio Grande and wiped out to the last man by a force of Rangers and deputies.[3] About ten years later, just when accounts of this Ranger exploit were getting into print, I remember seeing Aniceto Pizaña at a wedding on the south bank of the Rio Grande. He looked very much alive, and in 1954 I was told he was still living. Living too in the little towns on the south bank are a number of the Norias raiders.

It also seems a well-established fact that the Rangers often killed Mexicans who had nothing to do with the criminals they were after. Some actually were shot by mistake, according to the Ranger method of shooting first and asking questions afterwards.[4] But perhaps the majority of the innocent Mexicans who died at Ranger hands were killed much more deliberately than that. A wholesale butchery of "accomplices" was effected twice during Border history by the Rangers, after the Cortina uprising in 1859 and during the Pizaña uprising of 1915. Professor Webb calls the retaliatory killings of 1915 an "orgy of bloodshed [in which] the Texas Rangers played a prominent part."[5] He sets the number of Mexicans killed between 500 and 5,000. This was merely an intensification of an established practice which was carried on during less troubled years on a smaller scale.

Several motives must have been involved in the Ranger practice of killing innocent Mexicans as accomplices of the wrongdoers they could not catch. The most obvious one was "revenge by proxy," as Professor Webb calls it,[6] a precedent set by Bigfoot Wallace, who as a member of Hays's Rangers in the Mexican War killed as many inoffensive Mexicans as he could to avenge his imprisonment after the Mier expedition. A more practical motive was the fact that terror makes an occupied country submissive, something the Germans knew when they executed hostages in the occupied countries of Europe during World War II. A third motive may have been the Ranger weakness for sending impressive reports to Austin about their activities on the Border. The killing of innocent persons attracted unfavorable official notice only when it was extremely overdone.

In 1954 Mrs. Josefina Flores de Garza of Brownsville gave me some idea how it felt to be on the receiving end of the Ranger "orgy of bloodshed" of 1915. At that time Mrs. Garza was a girl of eighteen, the eldest of a family that included two younger boys in their teens and several small children. The family lived on a ranch near Harlingen, north of Brownsville. When the Ranger "executions" began, other Mexican ranchers sought refuge in town. The elder Flores refused to abandon his ranch, telling his children, "El que nada debe nada teme." (He who is guilty of nothing fears nothing.)

The Rangers arrived one day, surrounded the place and searched the outbuildings. The family waited in the house. Then the Rangers called the elder Flores out. He stepped to the door, and they shot him down. His two boys ran to him when he fell, and they were shot as they bent over their father. Then the Rangers came into the house and looked around. One of them saw a new pair of chaps, liked them, and took them with him. They left immediately afterwards.

From other sources I learned that the shock drove Josefina Flores temporarily insane. For two days her mother lived in the house with a brood of terrified youngsters, her deranged eldest daughter, and the corpses of her husband and her sons. Then a detachment of United States soldiers passed through, looking for raiders. They buried the bodies and got the family into town.

The daughter recovered her sanity after some time, but it still upsets her a great deal to talk about the killings. And, though forty years have passed, she still seems to be afraid that if she says something critical about the Rangers they will come and do her harm. Apparently Ranger terror did its work well, on the peaceful and the inoffensive.[7]

Except in the movies, ruthlessness and a penchant for stretching the truth do not in themselves imply a lack of courage. The Borderer's belief that all Rangers are shooters-in-the-back is of the same stuff as the Texan belief that all Mexicans are backstabbers. There is evidence, however, that not all Rangers lived up to their reputation as a fearless breed of men. Their basic techniques of ambush, surprise, and shooting first — with the resultant "mistake" killings of innocent bystanders — made them operate at times in ways that the average city policeman would be ashamed to imitate. The "shoot first and ask questions later" method of the Rangers has been romanticized into something dashing and daring, in technicolor, on a wide screen, and with Gary Cooper in the title role. Pierce's *Brief History* gives us an example of the way the method worked in actuality.

> On May 17, 1885, Sergt. B. D. Lindsay and six men from Company D frontier battalion of rangers, while scouting near the Rio Grande for escaped Mexican convicts, saw two Mexicans riding along. . . . As the horses suited the description of those alleged to be in possession of the convicts, and under the impression that these two were the men he was after, Lindsay called to them to halt, and at once opened fire on them. The elder Mexican fell to the ground with his horse, but the younger, firing from behind the dead animal, shot Private Sieker through the heart, killing him instantly. B. C. Reilly was shot through both thighs and badly wounded. The Mexicans stood their ground until the arrival of men from the ranch of a deputy-sheriff named Prudencio Herrera, who . . . insisted that the two Mexicans were well known and highly respected citizens and refused to turn them over to the rangers. . . . The citizens of Laredo . . . were indignant over the act of the rangers in shooting on Gonzalez, claiming that he was a well-known citizen of good repute, and alleging that the rangers would have killed them at the outset but for the fact that they defended themselves. The rangers, on the other hand, claimed that unless they would have proceeded as they did, should the Mexicans have been the criminals they were really after they, the rangers, would have been fired on first.[8]

There is unanswerable logic in the Ranger sergeant's argument, if one concedes him his basic premise: that a Mexican's life is of little value anyway. But this picture of seven Texas Rangers, feeling so defenseless in the face of two Mexicans that they must fire at them on sight, because the Mexicans might be mean and shoot at them first, is somewhat disillusioning to those of us who have grown up with the tradition of the lone Ranger getting off the train and telling the station hangers-on, "Of course they sent one Ranger. There's just one riot, isn't there?" Almost every week one reads of ordinary city policemen who capture desperate criminals — sometimes singlehandedly — without having to shoot first.

Sometimes the "shoot first" method led to even more serious consequences, and many a would-be Mexican-killer got his head blown off by a comrade who was eager to get in the first shot and mistook his own men for Mexicans while they all waited in ambush. Perhaps "shoot first and ask questions afterwards" is not the right name for this custom. "Shoot first and then see what you're shooting at" may be a better name. As such it has not been limited to the Texas Rangers. All over the United States during the deer season, Sunday hunters go out and shoot first.

Then there is the story about Alfredo Cerda, killed on Brownsville's main street in 1902. The Cerdas were prosperous ranchers near Brownsville, but it was their misfortune to live next to one of the "cattle barons" who was not through expanding yet. One day three Texas Rangers came down from Austin and "executed" the elder Cerda and one of his sons as cattle rustlers. The youngest son fled across the river, and thus the Cerda ranch was vacated. Five months later the remaining son, Alfredo Cerda, crossed over to Brownsville. He died the same day, shot down by a Ranger's gun.

Marcelo Garza, Sr., of Brownsville is no teller of folktales. He is a respected businessman, one of Brownsville's most highly regarded citizens of Mexican descent. Mr. Garza claims to have been an eyewitness to the shooting of the youngest Cerda. In 1902, Mr. Garza says, he was a clerk at the Tomás Fernández store on Elizabeth Street. A Ranger whom Mr. Garza identifies as "Bekar" shot Alfredo, Mr. Garza relates, as Cerda sat in the doorway of the Fernández store talking to Don Tomás, the owner. The Ranger used a rifle to kill Cerda, who was unarmed, "stalking him like a wild animal." After the shooting the Ranger ran into a nearby saloon, where other Rangers awaited him, and the group went out the back way and sought refuge with the federal troops in Fort Brown, to escape a mob of indignant citizens.[9] The same story had been told to me long before by my father, now deceased. He was not a witness to the shooting but claimed to have seen the chasing of the Rangers into Fort Brown.

Professor Webb mentions the shooting in 1902 of an Alfredo Cerda in Brownsville by Ranger A. Y. Baker. He gives no details.[10] Dobie also mentions an A. Y. Baker, "a famous ranger and sheriff of the border country," as the man responsible for the "extermination" of the unexterminated raiders of Norias.[11]

The methods of the Rangers are often justified as means to an end, the stamping out of lawlessness on the Border. This coin too has another face. Many Borderers will argue that the army and local law enforcement agencies were the ones that pacified the Border, that far from pacifying the area Ranger activities stirred it up, that instead of eliminating lawlessness along the Rio Grande the Rangers were for many years a primary cause of it. It is pointed out that it was the army that defeated the major border raiders and the local authorities that took care of thieves and smugglers. The notorious Lugo brothers were captured and executed by Cortina, the border raider. Mariano Reséndez, the famous smuggler, was taken by Mexican troops. Octaviano Zapata, the Union guerrilla leader during the Civil War, was defeated and slain by Texas-Mexican Confederates under Captain Antonio Benavides. After the Civil War, when released Confederate soldiers and lawless characters were disturbing the Border, citizens did not call for Rangers but organized a company of Texas-Mexicans under Captain Benavides to do their own pacifying.[12]

That the Rangers stirred up more trouble than they put down is an opinion that has been expressed by less partisan sources. Goldfinch quotes a Captain Ricketts of the United States Army, who was sent by the War Department to investigate Cortina's revolt, as saying that "conditions that brought federal troops to Brownsville had been nourished but not improved by demonstrations on the part of some Rangers and citizens."[13] In 1913 State Representative Cox of Ellis attempted to eliminate the Ranger force by striking out their appropriation from the budget. Cox declared "that there is more danger from the Rangers than from the men they are supposed to hunt down; that there is no authority of law for the Ranger force; that they are the most irresponsible officers in the State."[14] John Garner, future Vice-President of the United States, was among those who early in the twentieth century advocated abolishing the Ranger force.[15]

In *The Texas Rangers* Professor Webb notes that on the Border after 1848 the Mexican was "victimized by the law," that "the old landholding families found their titles in jeopardy and if they did not lose in the courts they lost to their American lawyers," and again that "the Mexicans suffered not only in their persons but in their property."[16] What he fails to note is that this lawless law was enforced principally by the Texas Rangers. It was the Rangers who could and did furnish the fortune-making adventurer with services not rendered by the United States Army or local sheriffs. And that is why from the point of view of the makers of fortunes the Rangers were so important to the "pacification" of the Border.

The Rangers and those who imitated their methods undoubtedly exacerbated the cultural conflict on the Border rather than allayed it. The assimilation of the north-bank Border people into the American commonwealth was necessary to any effective pacification of the Border. Ranger operations did much to impede that end. They created in the Border Mexican a deep and understandable hostility for American authority; they drew Border communities even closer together than they had been, though at that time they were beginning to disintegrate under the impact of new conditions.

Terror cowed the more inoffensive Mexican, but it also added to the roll of bandits and raiders many high-spirited individuals who would have otherwise remained peaceful and useful citizens. These were the heroes of the Border folk. People sang *corridos* about these men who, in the language of the ballads, "each with his pistol defended his right."

NOTES

1. Charles William Goldfinch, *Juan N. Cortina: Two Interpretations* (Arno Press, 1974), p. 49.
2. *Ibid.*, p. 62.
3. J. Frank Dobie, "Versos of the Texas Vaqueros," *Publications of the Texas Folklore Society*, IV, Austin, 1925, p. 32.
4. See Walter Prescott Webb, *The Texas Rangers* (University of Texas Press, 1965), pp. 263ff., for an account of one of these "mistake" slaughters of all adult males in a peaceful ranchero community on the Mexican side, by McNelly.
5. *Ibid.*, p. 478.
6. *Ibid.*, p. 87.
7. In *A Brief History of the Lower Rio Grande Valley*, Menasha (Wisconsin), 1917, p. 90, Frank Cushman Pierce reports: "On August 3, 1915, rangers and deputy sheriffs attacked a ranch near Paso Real, about 32 miles north of Brownsville, and killed Desiderio Flores and his two sons, Mexicans, alleged to be bandits."
8. Frank C. Pierce, *A Brief History of the Lower Rio Grande Valley* (Menasha, WI: The Collegiate Press/George Banta Publishing Company, 1917), pp. 110–111.
9. Letter of Marcelo Garza, Sr., to the author, dated July 7, 1955, and subsequent conversation with Mr. Garza in Brownsville, December 29, 1957.
10. Webb, *The Texas Rangers*, p. 464.
11. Dobie, "Versos of the Texas Vaqueros," p. 32.

12. Annie Cowling, *The Civil War Trade of the Lower Rio Grande Valley*, Master's thesis, University of Texas, 1926, pp. 136ff.
13. Goldfinch, *Juan N. Cortina*, p. 48.
14. San Antonio *Express*, July 29, 1913, p. 3.
15. Sequin *Enterprise*, April 18, 1902, p. 2.
16. Webb, *The Texas Rangers*, pp. 175-176.

QUESTIONS FOR CRITICAL THINKING AND WRITING

1. Paredes's essay provides both anecdotal evidence and a number of first-hand accounts. Do these accounts illustrate Paredes's argument? How? How do they influence your opinion of the Rangers?

2. Do you believe an attitude of "shoot first, ask questions later" is ever justifiable? Why or why not? How does Paredes feel about the Rangers' policy?

3. Paredes includes a list of Border Mexican sayings about the Rangers. Would familiar expressions like those have been accepted as truths? What do the sayings indicate about local attitudes toward the Rangers?

4 Paredes writes, "Terror cowed the more inoffensive Mexican, but it also added to the roll of bandits and raiders many high-spirited individuals who would have otherwise remained peaceful and useful citizens." What do you think he means? In an essay, explain the role of terror as conveyed in Paredes's writing in the lives of soldiers, law enforcers, and civilians living on the early Texas frontier. According to Paredes, what were some of the consequences of the Rangers' tactics?

KATHERINE ANNE PORTER

Papers of Katherine Anne Porter, Special Collections, University of Maryland Libraries.

Katherine Anne Porter (1890–1980) was a journalist, essayist, novelist, and short story writer. Born Callie Russell Porter in Indian Creek, Texas, she later lived in Kyle, Texas, and attended school from 1904 to 1905 in San Antonio. She married four times, and her fourth husband, Albert Erskine, was the business manager for the *Southern Review*. "The Grave" is the first of several stories she wrote featuring the protagonist Miranda — these stories are said to have some parallels with Porter's own life. "I shall try to tell the truth," said Porter of her work, "but the result will be fiction." Best known for her short stories, Porter was a prolific writer whose works included *Ship of Fools* (novel); *Flowering Judas and Other Stories*; *Pale Horse, Pale Rider*; *Noon Wine*; *The Old Order: Stories of the South*; *The Never-Ending Wrong*; *The Collected Essays and Occasional Writings of Katherine Anne Porter*; and some poetry.

BEFORE YOU READ

In the following story, nine-year-old Miranda is out having an adventure with her brother Paul. Many years later, Miranda recalls that day and their unexpected findings. What is the significance of what Miranda discovers? How does the discovery affect her?

The Grave   1935

The grandfather, dead for more than thirty years, had been twice disturbed in his long repose by the constancy and possessiveness of his widow. She removed his bones first to Louisiana and then to Texas as if she had set out to find her own burial place, knowing well she would never return to the places she had left. In Texas she set up a small cemetery in a corner of her first farm, and as the family connection grew, and oddments of relations came over from Kentucky to settle, it contained at last about twenty graves. After the grandmother's death, part of her land was to be sold for the benefit of certain of her children, and the cemetery happened to lie in the part set aside for sale. It was necessary to take up the bodies and bury them again in the family plot in the big new public cemetery, where the grandmother had been buried. At last her husband was to lie beside her for eternity, as she had planned.

The family cemetery had been a pleasant small neglected garden of tangled rose bushes and ragged cedar trees and cypress, the simple flat stones rising out of uncropped sweet-smelling wild grass. The graves were lying open and empty one burning day when Miranda and her brother Paul, who often went together to hunt rabbits and doves, propped their .22 Winchester rifles carefully against the rail fence, climbed over and explored among the graves. She was nine years old and he was twelve.

They peered into the pits all shaped alike with such purposeful accuracy, and looking at each other with pleased adventurous eyes, they said in solemn tones: "These were graves!" trying by words to shape a special, suitable emotion in their minds, but they felt nothing except an agreeable thrill of wonder: they were seeing a new sight, doing something they had not done before. In them both there was also a small disappointment at the entire commonplaceness of the actual spectacle. Even if it had once contained a coffin for years upon years, when the coffin was gone a grave was just a hole in the ground. Miranda leaped into the pit that had held her grandfather's bones. Scratching around aimlessly and pleasurably as any young animal, she scooped up a lump of earth and weighed it in her palm. It had a pleasantly sweet, corrupt smell, being mixed with cedar needles and small leaves, and as the crumbs fell apart, she saw a silver dove no larger than a hazel nut, with spread wings and a neat fan-shaped tail. The breast had a deep round hollow in it. Turning it up to the fierce sunlight, she saw that the inside of the hollow was cut in little whorls. She scrambled out, over the pile of loose earth that had fallen back into the end of the grave, calling to Paul that she had found something, he must guess what. His head appeared smiling over the rim of another grave. He waved a closed hand at her. "I've got something too!" They ran to compare treasures, making a game of it, so many guesses each, all wrong, and a final showdown with opened palms. Paul had found a thin wide gold ring carved with intricate flowers and leaves. Miranda was smitten at sight of the ring and wished to have it. Paul seemed more impressed by the dove. They made a trade, with some little bickering. After he had got the dove in his hand, Paul said, "Don't you know what this is? This is a screw head for a *coffin*! . . . I'll bet nobody else in the world has one like this!"

Miranda glanced at it without covetousness. She had the gold ring on her thumb; it fitted perfectly. "Maybe we ought to go now," she said, "maybe one of the niggers 'll see us and tell somebody." They knew the land had been sold, the cemetery was no longer theirs, and they felt like trespassers. They climbed back over the fence, slung their rifles loosely under their arms — they had been shooting at targets with various kinds of firearms since they were seven years old — and set out to look for the rabbits and doves or whatever small game might happen along. On these expeditions Miranda always followed at Paul's heels along the path, obeying instructions about handling her gun when going through fences; learning how to stand it up properly so it would not slip and fire unexpectedly; how to wait her time for a shot and not just bang away in the air without looking, spoiling shots for Paul, who really could hit things if given a chance. Now and then, in her excitement at seeing birds whizz up suddenly before her face, or a rabbit leap across her very toes, she lost her head, and almost without sighting she flung her rifle up and pulled the trigger. She hardly ever hit any sort of mark. She had no proper sense of hunting at all. Her brother would be often completely disgusted with her. "You don't care whether you get your bird or not," he said. "That's no way to hunt." Miranda could not understand his indignation. She had seen him smash his hat and yell with fury when he had missed his aim. "What I like about shooting," said Miranda, with exasperating inconsequence, "is pulling the trigger and hearing the noise."

"Then, by golly," said Paul, "why'n't you go back to the range and shoot at bulls-eyes?"

"I'd just as soon," said Miranda, "only like this, we walk around more."

"Well, you just stay behind and stop spoiling my shots," said Paul, who, when he made a kill, wanted to be certain he had made it. Miranda, who alone brought down a bird once in twenty rounds, always claimed as her own any game they got when they fired at the same moment. It was tiresome and unfair and her brother was sick of it.

"Now, the first dove we see, or the first rabbit, is mine," he told her. "And the next will be yours. Remember that and don't get smarty."

"What about snakes?" asked Miranda idly. "Can I have the first snake?"

Waving her thumb gently and watching her gold ring glitter, Miranda lost interest in shooting. She was wearing her summer roughing outfit: dark blue overalls, a light blue shirt, a hired-man's straw hat, and thick brown sandals. Her brother had the same outfit except his was a sober hickory-nut color. Ordinarily Miranda preferred her overalls to any other dress, though it was making rather a scandal in the countryside, for the year was 1903, and in the back country the law of female decorum had teeth in it. Her father had been criticized for letting his girls dress like boys and go careering around astride barebacked horses. Big sister Maria, the really independent and fearless one, in spite of her rather affected ways, rode at a dead run with only a rope knotted around her horse's nose. It was said the motherless family was running down, with the Grandmother no longer there to hold it together. It was known that she had discriminated against her son Harry in her will, and that he was in straits about money. Some of his old neighbors reflected with vicious satisfaction that now he would probably not be so stiffnecked, nor have any more high-stepping horses either. Miranda knew this, though she could not say how. She had met along the road old women of the kind who smoked corn-cob pipes, who had treated her grandmother with most sincere respect. They slanted their gummy old eyes side-ways at the granddaughter and said, "Ain't you ashamed of yoself, Missy? It's aginst the Scriptures to dress like that. Whut yo Pappy thinkin about?" Miranda, with her powerful social sense, which was like a fine set of antennae radiating from every pore of her skin, would feel ashamed because she knew well it was rude and ill-bred to shock anybody, even bad-tempered old crones, though she had faith in her father's judgment and was perfectly comfortable in the clothes. Her father had said. "They're just what you need, and they'll save your dresses for school . . ." This sounded quite simple and natural to her. She had been brought up in rigorous economy. Wastefulness was vulgar. It was also a sin. These were truths; she had heard them repeated many times and never once disputed.

Now the ring, shining with the serene purity of fine gold on her rather grubby thumb, turned her feelings against her overalls and sockless feet, toes sticking through the thick brown leather straps. She wanted to go back to the farmhouse, take a good cold bath, dust herself with plenty of Maria's violet talcum powder — provided Maria was not present to object, of course — put on the thinnest, most becoming dress she owned, with a big sash, and sit in a wicker chair under the trees . . . These things were not all she wanted, of course; she had vague stirrings of desire for luxury and a grand way of living which could not take precise form in her imagination but were founded on family legend of past wealth and leisure. These immediate comforts were what she could have, and she wanted them at once. She lagged rather far behind Paul, and once she thought of just turning back without a word and going home. She stopped, thinking that Paul would never do that to her, and so she would have to tell him. When a rabbit leaped, she let Paul have it without dispute. He killed it with one shot.

When she came up with him, he was already kneeling, examining the wound, the rabbit trailing from his hands. "Right through the head," he said complacently, as if he had aimed for it. He took out his sharp, competent bowie knife and started to skin the body. He did it very cleanly and quickly. Uncle Jimbilly knew how to prepare the skins so that Miranda always had fur coats for her dolls, for though she never cared much for her dolls she liked seeing them in fur coats. The children knelt facing each other over the dead animal. Miranda watched admiringly while her brother stripped the skin away as if he were taking off a glove. The flayed flesh emerged dark scarlet, sleek, firm; Miranda with thumb and finger felt the long fine muscles with the silvery flat strips binding them to the joints. Brother lifted the oddly bloated belly. "Look," he said, in a low amazed voice. "It was going to have young ones."

Very carefully he slit the thin flesh from the center ribs to the flanks, and a scarlet bag appeared. He slit again and pulled the bag open, and there lay a bundle of tiny rabbits, each wrapped in a thin scarlet veil. The brother pulled these off and there they were, dark gray, their sleek wet down lying in minute even ripples, like a baby's head just washed, their unbelievably small delicate ears folded close, their little blind faces almost featureless.

Miranda said, "Oh, I want to *see*," under her breath. She looked and looked—excited but not frightened, for she was accustomed to the sight of animals killed in hunting—filled with pity and astonishment and a kind of shocked delight in the wonderful little creatures for their own sakes, they were so pretty. She touched one of them ever so carefully, "Ah, there's blood running over them," she said and began to tremble without knowing why. Yet she wanted most deeply to see and to know. Having seen, she felt at once as if she had known all along. The very memory of her former ignorance faded, she had always known just this. No one had ever told her anything outright, she had been rather unobservant of the animal life around her because she was so accustomed to animals. They seemed simply disorderly and unaccountably rude in their habits, but altogether natural and not very interesting. Her brother had spoken as if he had known about everything all along. He may have seen all this before. He had never said a word to her, but she knew now a part at least of what he knew. She understood a little of the secret, formless intuitions in her own mind and body, which had been clearing up, taking form, so gradually and so steadily she had not realized that she was learning what she had to know. Paul said cautiously, as if he were talking about something forbidden: "They were just about ready to be born." His voice dropped on the last word. "I know," said Miranda, "like kittens. I know, like babies." She was quietly and terribly agitated, standing again with her rifle under her arm, looking down at the bloody heap. "I don't want the skin," she said, "I won't have it." Paul buried the young rabbits again in their mother's body, wrapped the skin around her, carried her to a clump of sage bushes, and hid her away. He came out again at once and said to Miranda, with an eager friendliness, a confidential tone quite unusual in him, as if he were taking her into an important secret on equal terms: "Listen now. Now you listen to me, and don't ever forget. Don't you ever tell a living soul that you saw this. Don't tell a soul. Don't tell Dad because I'll get into trouble. He'll say I'm leading you into things you ought not to do. He's always saying that. So now don't you go and forget and blab out sometime the way you're always doing . . . Now, that's a secret. Don't you tell."

Miranda never told, she did not even wish to tell anybody. She thought about the whole worrisome affair with confused unhappiness for a few days. Then it sank quietly into her mind and was heaped over by accumulated thousands of impressions, for nearly twenty years. One day she was picking her path among the puddles and crushed refuse of a market street in a strange city of a strange country, when without warning, plain and clear in its true colors as if she looked through a frame upon a scene that had not stirred nor changed since the moment it happened, the episode of that far-off day leaped from its burial place before her mind's eye. She was so reasonlessly horrified she halted suddenly staring, the scene before her eyes dimmed by the vision back of them. An Indian vendor had held up before her a tray of dyed sugar sweets, in the shapes of all kinds of small creatures: birds, baby chicks, baby rabbits, lambs, baby pigs. They were in gay colors and smelled of vanilla, maybe. . . . It was a very hot day and the smell in the market, with its piles of raw flesh and wilting flowers, was like the mingled sweetness and corruption she had smelled that other day in the empty cemetery at home: the day she had remembered always until now vaguely as the time she and her brother had found treasure in the opened graves. Instantly upon this thought the dreadful vision faded, and she saw clearly her brother, whose childhood face she had forgotten, standing again in the blazing sunshine, again twelve years old, a pleased sober smile in his eyes, turning the silver dove over and over in his hands.

QUESTIONS FOR CRITICAL THINKING AND WRITING

1. What can you tell about the lives of the characters in this family, based on Porter's descriptions of them? Support your insights with specific passages from the text.

2. How does Miranda feel about herself when she's wearing the ring? What things does she long for that hadn't occurred to her before?

3. Porter says of Miranda, "she knew now a part at least of what he knew" after seeing her older brother Paul holding the dead rabbits. What do you think that means?

4. Titles often connect to a main theme or idea in a work. Why is this story titled "The Grave"? Go beyond the obvious reference to the grandfather's grave in the opening paragraph, and write an essay exploring the meanings behind Porter's title.

ROBERT PENN WARREN

Robert Penn Warren (1905-1989) was a poet, novelist, and critic who was associated with a group of Southern writers known as the Fugitive Poets. Born in Kentucky, he attended Vanderbilt University, the University of California, Berkeley, Yale University, and Oxford (as a Rhodes Scholar). He is best known for his novel *All the King's Men,* which won the Pulitzer Prize in 1947, and he won Pulitzers for his poetry in 1957 and 1979. The following reading is from Warren's eulogy for the author Katherine Anne Porter.

BEFORE YOU READ

In his accolades for Katherine Anne Porter, Warren explains the process by which her work achieves its particular voice and style. After reading her story "The Grave" and then this commentary, do you get a sense of the Katherine Anne Porter described here? Of what Warren describes as her "precision of language" and of the "revealing shock of precise observation" in Porter's work?

On Katherine Anne Porter 1980

Pondering [the] extraordinary accumulation of [her] spontaneous and unpublished material, one is tempted to suggest that for Katherine Anne Porter the distinction between art and life was never arbitrarily drawn: Life found its fulfillment in the thrust toward art, and art sprang from life as realized in meditation. In an interview with Hank Lopez, she once said: "Everything I ever wrote in the way of fiction is based very securely in something in real life." Eudora Welty sensed this about her friend when she wrote, "What we are responding to in Katherine Anne Porter's work is the intensity of its life.". . .

No exploration of Katherine Anne Porter's "personality" . . . can explain the success of her art: the scrupulous and expressive intricacy of structure, the combination of a precision of language, the revealing shock of precise observation and organic metaphor, a vital rhythmic felicity of style, and a significant penetration of a governing idea into the remotest details of a work. If, as V. S. Pritchett has put it, the writer of short stories is concerned with "one thing that implies many" — or much — then we have here a most impressive artist.

How did Katherine Anne Porter transmute life finally into art? In her journal of 1936, she herself provided a most succinct, simple, and precise answer to my question. All her experience, she writes, seems to be simply in memory, with continuity, marginal notes, constant revision and comparison of one thing with another. But now comes the last phase, that of ultimate transmutation: "Now and again, thousands of memories converge, harmonize, arrange themselves around a central idea in a coherent form, and I write a story."

The author here speaks as though each story were an isolated creation, called into being by the initial intuition of a theme. That, indeed, may have been her immediate perception of the process of composition. The work of any serious writer, however, is not a grab bag, but a struggle, conscious or unconscious, for a meaningful unity, a unity that can be recorded in terms of temperament or theme. In my view, the final importance of Katherine Anne Porter is not merely that she has written a number of fictions remarkable for both grace and strength, a number of fictions which have enlarged and deepened the nature of the story, both short and long, in our time, but that she has created an *oeuvre* — a body of work including fiction, essays, letters, and journals — that bears the stamp of a personality distinctive, . . . and thoroughly committed to a quest for meaning in the midst of the ironic complexities of man's lot.

QUESTIONS FOR CRITICAL THINKING AND WRITING

1. To what extent is Warren's description of Porter and her work persuasive? What do you see in Porter's story "The Grave" (p. 140) that supports (or refutes) Warren's observations?

2. Explain the difference between Porter's explanation of how she writes and Warren's commentary on her work, found in the last two paragraphs of Warren's essay.

3. Does Warren view Porter's writing as particularly Texan? How does the Warren commentary on Porter connect with Larry McMurtry's commentary (p. 116) on what writers should write about?

THE STATE OF TEXAS

The revolutionary war for Mexican independence from Spain began in 1810. Soon after, Texas became embroiled in the resulting unrest. Revolutionary José Bernardo Gutiérrez de Lara began to advocate for the "liberation of Texas" from Spain and gained support from the U.S. government in Washington and from other Spanish-speaking and Anglo Texans. Gutiérrez and his men captured San Antonio in 1813 and issued a "Declaration of Independence" and "First Constitution" shortly thereafter. The constitution provided for a government for "the State of Texas, forming part of the Mexican Republic," as Gutiérrez wrote, rather than an independent Texas, as some Texans had hoped for. The following early documents are the basis of government for what is known as the First Republic of Texas. It was not until 1836 that Texas became independent of Mexico.

BEFORE YOU READ

The Texas Declaration of Independence and first Constitution were drawn up to declare Texas's independence from Spain and to structure the government of the newly formed Republic of Texas. What do you know about this part of Texas history? Why might such documents be necessary during a time of unrest for a country, a state, or a region? What are the main arguments of these documents? Who were they meant to persuade — and why?

From *The Declaration of Independence, April 6, 1813*

Mexico began its long struggle for independence in 1810. The revolution shortly spread to Texas. The initial revolt in 1811 at San Antonio was premature, but a more formidable moment, led by José Bernardo Gutiérrez de Lara, developed the next year. Gutiérrez, as an envoy of the Mexican revolutionists, had failed to gain official recognition by the United States, but he had found public sentiment in Natchitoches, New Orleans, and Washington highly favorable towards Mexican independence. Thereupon, he set up headquarters in the Neutral Ground, flooded Texas with propaganda advocating a new order along the lines of the current liberal philosophies, and got an ex-United States Army officer, Augustus W. Magee, to join him in raising the "Republican Army of the North" for the purpose of liberating Texas. Entering Texas on August 8, 1812, the revolutionists advanced to Nacogdoches, where they were received with great enthusiasm, the royalist troops deserting to their forces. They captured San Fernando de Béxar (San Antonio) without difficulty on April 1, 1813, where five days later the leaders issued a Declaration of Independence, a document obviously inspired by that of the United States.
—From Documents of Texas History, *edited by Ernest Wallace et al.*

We, the people of the province of Texas, calling on the Supreme Judge of the Universe to witness the rectitude of our intentions, declare, that the ties which held us under the domination of Spain and Europe, are forever dissolved; that we possess the right to establish a government for ourselves; that in the future all legitimate authority shall emanate from the people to whom alone it rightfully belongs, and that henceforth all allegiance or subjection to any foreign power whatsoever, is entirely renounced.

A relation of the causes which have conduced to render this step necessary, is due to our dignity, and to the opinion of the world. A long series of occurrences, originating in the weakness and corruption of the Spanish rulers, has converted that monarchy into the theatre of a sanguinary war, between two contending powers, itself destined the prize of the victor; a king in the power and subject to the authority of one of them, the miserable wreck of its government in the possession of the other, it appears to have lost the substance of any form of sovereignty. — Unable to defend itself on the Peninsula, much less to protect its distant colonies; those colonies are abandoned to the caprice of wicked men, whilst there exists no power to which they may be made responsible for the abuse of their authority, or for the consequence of their rapacity. Self preservation, the highest law of nature, if no other motive, would have justified this step. But, independent of this necessity, a candid world will acknowledge that we have had cause amply sufficient, in the sufferings and oppression which we have so long endured.

Governments are established for the good of communities of men, and not for the benefit and aggrandisement of individuals. When these ends are perverted to a system of oppression, the people have a right to change them for a better, and for such as may be best adapted to their situation. Man is formed in the image of his Creator: he sins who submits to slavery. Who will say that our sufferings are not such as to have driven us to the farthest bounds of patience, and to justify us in establishing a new government, and in choosing new rulers to whom we may intrust our happiness?

We were governed by insolent strangers, who regarded their authority only as a means of enriching themselves by the plunder of those whom they were sent to govern, while we had no participation either in national or municipal affairs.

We feel with indignation, the unheard of tyranny of being excluded from all communication with other nations, which might tend to improve our situation, physical and moral. We were prohibited the use of books, of speech, and even of thought — our country was our prison. . . .

From *The First Constitution, April 17, 1813*

On April 17 Gutiérrez and the junta at San Antonio issued the first constitution of Texas. The constitution provided for a Spanish-type government for "the State of Texas, forming a part of the Mexican Republic." Disappointed over this reactionary development, the liberals lost interest, and, shortly afterwards, when the Republican forces were defeated by General Joaquín de Arredondo, commandant of the Eastern Interior Provinces, on the Medina River near San Antonio, the first independent Texas movement collapsed. Gutiérrez sent a manuscript copy (in Spanish) of his "Constitution of the State of Texas" to William Shaler, Special Agent of the United States stationed at Natchitoches to observe developments in Texas, who in turn enclosed it in his report of May 14, 1813, to Secretary of State James Monroe. It is from this copy that the English translation reproduced here is taken.
— *From* Documents of Texas History, *edited by Ernest Wallace et al.*

1. The province of Texas shall henceforth be known only as the State of Texas, forming part of the Mexican Republic, to which it remains inviolably joined.

2. Our Holy Religion will remain unchanged in the way it is now established, and the laws will be duly executed unless they are expressly and publicly revoked or altered in the manner herein prescribed.

3. Private property and possessions will be inviolable, and will never be taken for public use except in urgent cases of necessity, in which instances the proprietor will be duly compensated.

4. From today henceforward personal liberty will be held sacred. No man will be arrested for any crime without a formal accusation made in the proper form under oath being first presented. No man will be placed before the Tribunal without first having been examined by the witnesses. Neither will any man be deprived of life without having been heard completely [in court], an exception being made from this rule during the time of the present War in the case of criminals of the Republic, whose punishments will be decided by the Junta in accord with the Governor in order to assure the firmness of an Establishment and to protect the people.

5. The Governor selected by the Junta will be Commander-in Chief of the military forces of the State, but he will undertake no campaign personally without having received the order of the Junta. In such a case, the Governor will provide the necessary means for maintaining the obligations of Government during his absence. Also under his charge will be the establishment of laws pertaining to the organization of the Army, the naming of military officials, and the ratifying of the commissions and ranks of those already employed. He shall be intrusted with the defense of the Country, foreign relations, execution of the laws, and preservation of order. He will have a right to one secretary, two aides-de-camp, three clerks for the Spanish language and one for English. . . .

— City of San Fernando, April 17, 1813

QUESTIONS FOR CRITICAL THINKING AND WRITING

1. What similarities does the Texas Declaration of Independence of 1813 share with the U.S. Declaration of Independence penned in 1776? Are they comparable?

2. Given what you've read here, how does the Texas Constitution clarify the function of Texas government and provide for the protection of the people of Texas?

3. How is the drafting of the Texas Declaration of Independence an act of "self preservation" for Texans?

4. **RESEARCH AND WRITE.** Before the Republic of Texas's annexation by the United States, Texans had ties to Mexico and were affected by the Mexican War of Independence. Research the conflict that led to the writing of the first Texas Declaration of Independence and Constitution. Write a brief essay that outlines the major events leading up to them and the effects, if any, their existence has had on the state.

Acknowledgments (continued from p. ii)

Sandra Cisneros. "Woman Hollering Creek" from *Woman Hollering Creek*. Copyright © 1991 by Sandra Cisneros. Published by Vintage Books, a division of Random House, Inc., New York, and originally in hardcover by Random House, Inc. Reprinted by permission of Susan Bergholz Literary Services, New York, NY and Lamy, NM. All rights reserved.

J. Frank Dobie. Excerpt from "W. W. Burton, An Old Trail Driver Tells His Story" edited, from *Out of the Old Rock by J. Frank Dobie*. Copyright © 1955, 1962, 1966, 1972 by Bertha Dobie. Published by Little, Brown and Company. Reprinted by permission of the Hachette Book Group.

Dagoberto Gilb. "Truck" from *The Magic of Blood*. Reprinted by permission of the author.

Don Graham. Edited selection from "Introduction" from *Lone Star Literature*, edited by Don Graham. Copyright © 2003 by Don Graham. Used by permission of W. W. Norton & Company, Inc.

Christine Granados. "The Bride" from *Brides and Sinners in El Chuco: Short Stories* by Christine Granados. Copyright © 2006 by Christine Granados. Reprinted by permission of The University of Arizona Press.

John Graves. Excerpt from *Goodbye to a River* by John Graves. Copyright © 1960. Alfred A. Knopf.

Macarena Hernández. "One Family, Two Homelands: Big City Girl," reprinted by permission of Macarena Hernández.

Rolando Hinojosa-Smith. "Night Burial Details" from *Korean Love Songs* by Rolando Hinojosa-Smith. Bilingual Review Press. Copyright © 1992. Reprinted by permission of Rolando Hinojosa-Smith.

Molly Ivins. Excerpt from "Is Texas America?" in *The Nation*, November 17, 2003. Copyright The Estate of Mary T. Ivins. Reprinted by permission of Pom, Inc., New York. "Texas Women: True Grit and All the Rest" from *Molly Ivins Can't Say That Can She?* by Molly Ivins, copyright © 1991 by Molly Ivins. Used by permission of Random House, Inc.

Barbara Jordan. Excerpt from Barbara Jordan's Keynote Address to the Democratic National Convention, July 13, 1992, reprinted by permission of Texas Southern University.

Mary Karr. "Chapter 7 – Texas 1961" from *The Liars' Club* by Mary Karr, copyright © 1995 by Mary Karr. Used by permission of Viking Penguin, a division of Penguin Group (USA) Inc.

Larry McMurtry. Excerpt from *The Last Picture Show* by Larry McMurtry, and excerpts from "An Introduction: The God Abandons Texas" from *In a Narrow Grave: Essays on Texas* by Larry McMurtry, copyright © 1994, 1996 by Larry McMurtry. Reprinted with permission of The Wylie Agency LLC.

Harryette Mullen. "Las Locas" and "Momma Sayings" from *Blues Baby: Early Poems* by Harryette Mullen. University of Arizona Press. Copyright © 2002 by Harryette Mullen. Reprinted by permission.

Native American Tribes of Texas. Tejas (Hasinai) Tribe, "The Beginning of the World"; Caddo Tribe, "Coyote and the Seven Brothers"; Kiowa-Apache Tribe, "Coyote Makes the Sun"; Kiowa-Apache Tribe, "How Poor Boy Won his Wife," reprinted with the permission of Margaret K. McElderry Books, an imprint of Simon & Schuster Children's Publishing Division from *Hold Up the Sky* Retold by Jane Louise Curry. Text copyright © 2003 Jane Louise Curry.

Naomi Shihab Nye. "Hello" and "Famous" from *Words Under the Words: Selected Poems* by Naomi Shihab Nye. Copyright © 1995 by Naomi Shihab Nye. Far Corner Books. Reprinted by permission of the author.

Américo Paredes. Excerpt "The Texas Rangers" from "Chapter I – The Country," from *With His Pistol in His Hand: A Border Ballad and Its Hero* by Américo Paredes, Copyright © 1958, renewed 1986. Reprinted by permission of the University of Texas Press.

Katherine Anne Porter. "The Grave" from *The Leaning Tower and Other Stories*, copyright 1944 and renewed 1972 by Katherine Anne Porter. Reprinted by permission of Houghton Mifflin Harcourt Publishing Company.

Walter Prescott Webb. Excerpt from *The Great Plains* by Walter Prescott Webb. Copyright © 1931, 1959 by Walter Prescott Webb. Reprinted by permission of Pearson Education, Inc. All Rights Reserved.

Index of Authors and Titles

Students, need help with your writing?

Visit the *Re:Writing* Web site

bedfordstmartins.com/rewriting

Re:Writing is a comprehensive Web site designed to help you with the most common writing concerns. You'll find advice from experts, models you can rely on, and exercises that will tell you right away how you're doing. And it's all free and available any hour of the day. You can find help for the following situations at the specific areas of **bedfordstmartins.com/rewriting** listed below.

- Need help with grammar problems?   **Exercise Central**

- Stuck somewhere in the research process? (Maybe at the beginning?)   **The Bedford Research Room**

- Wondering whether a Web site is good enough to use in your paper?   **Evaluating Online Sources Tutorial**

- Having trouble figuring out how to cite a source?   **Research and Documentation Online**

- Need help creating the Works Cited page for your research paper?   **The Bedford Bibliographer**

- Confused about plagiarism?   **Avoiding Plagiarism Tutorial**

- Want to get more out of your word processor?   **Using Your Word Processor**

- Trying to improve the look of your paper?   **Designing Documents with a Word Processor**

- Need to create slides for a presentation?   **Preparing Presentation Slides Tutorial**

- Interested in creating a Web site?   **Mike Markel's Web Design Tutorial**